Grammar Works
Student's Book

1

Mick Gammidge

CAMBRIDGE
UNIVERSITY PRESS

PUBLISHED BY THE PRESS SYNDICATE OF THE UNIVERSITY OF CAMBRIDGE
The Pitt Building, Trumpington Street, Cambridge CB2 1RP, United Kingdom

CAMBRIDGE UNIVERSITY PRESS
The Edinburgh Building, Cambridge CB2 2RU, United Kingdom
40 West 20th Street, New York, NY 10011-4211, USA
10 Stamford Road, Oakleigh, Melbourne 3166, Australia

First published 1998

Printed in the United Kingdom at the University Press, Cambridge

ISBN 0 521 555426 Student's Book 1
ISBN 0 521 55540X Teacher's Book 1

Contents

1 Hello. You're new here

1a Read the conversation.

Hello. You're new here. I'm Sue.

... and she's Linda.

Uhh!

I'm sorry. They're not happy today.

No, we're not!

But it's not friendly. Sorry!

Yes. Hello, Sue. I'm Eric – and he's Mark ...

Hello.

Er ... it's beautiful.

Ahhrrgh!

b Write the words below.

1 _____

2 _____

3 she

4 _____

5 _____

6 _____

7 you

8 _____

9 _____

10 they

2 Complete the chart.

1	I am = _____	you are = _____	he is = _____	she is = _____	it is = _____
2+	we are = we're	you are = _____		they are = _____	

CHECK THE ANSWERS ON PAGE 60.

3 Write sentences.

1 I'm hungry.

2 _____ 's busy.

3 _____ 're ill.

4 _____ tall.

5 _____ 're 13.

6 _____ expensive.

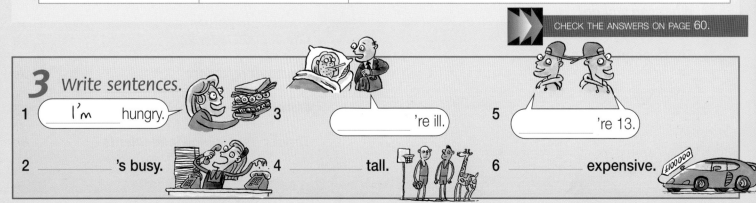

4a Look at exercise 1 again. Complete the sentences.

It's beautiful.

It _____ friendly.

They _____ happy.

b Match the words below.

I	she we	we
	he it	you they

'm not	aren't	am not	's not

're not	isn't	are not	is not

CHECK THE ANSWERS AND STUDY THE CHARTS ON PAGE 60.

5 Right (✓) or wrong (✗)?

1 It's fast. ✗

2 He isn't happy. ☐

3 They're old. ☐

4 They aren't hot. ☐

5 It isn't dirty. ☐

6 She isn't tired. ☐

7 They're not busy. ☐

6 Correct the wrong sentences in exercise 5.

1 It isn't fast. It's slow.

2 He's happy.

3 ☐ _____

4 ☐ _____

5 ☐ _____

6 ☐ _____

7 Write sentences about you. Use the words below.

1 tall   2 happy   3 tired   4 old
5 hungry   6 hot   7 busy

Examples:

I'm tall./I'm not tall./I'm not tall. I'm short.

1 _____
2 _____
3 _____
4 _____
5 _____
6 _____
7 _____

PUZZLE

Argument!

One person is right. Two are wrong.
Complete the sentence.

LINDA: I'm right.

MARK: You're wrong, Eric.

ERIC: You're not right, Linda.

_____ is right.

2 Who are you?

1a Read the cartoon.
b Look at the sentences and make questions.

You	are	crazy.
Are	you	crazy?

You	are	OK.

He	is	Spider Boy.
Who	is	he?

She	is	Cat Girl.

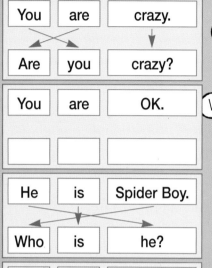

Who are you?

I'm Cat Girl.

Oh! And who am I?

You're Lion Boy. Are you OK?

Yes, I am.

Who is he? Is he crazy?

No, he isn't! He's Spider Boy!

Oh, no! Who are they?

2 Complete the charts.

Who	am	I?
		she? he? it?
		we? you? they?

		I
		she he it
		we you they

tall? new? crazy?

Yes,	I	.
	she he it	.
	we you they	.

No,	I	.
	she he it	.
	we you they	.

3 Put the words in the correct order. Make questions.

1 | strong | is | Lion Boy |
Is Lion Boy strong?

2 | crazy | Spider Boy | is |
_____

3 | is | brave | Cat Girl |
_____

4 | Spider Boy | old | Cat Girl | and | are |
_____

5 | are | and | clever |
| Lion Boy | Spider Boy |
_____

6 | stupid | Cat Girl | is |
_____

CHECK THE ANSWERS AND STUDY THE CHARTS ON PAGE 61.

4 Write short answers for the questions in exercise 3.

1 Yes, he is.
2 _____
3 _____
4 _____
5 _____
6 _____

5 Write questions and answers.

1 Who is he?
  He's Batman.

2 _____

3 _____

4 _____

5 _____

6 _____

Tom & Jerry
© 1998 Turner Entertainment Co.

Björk

6 Complete the conversation.

FRANK: Hello, (1) _____ Frank.
         (2) _____ are (3) _____ ?
MRS W: (4) _____ Mrs White.
FRANK: (5) _____ beautiful!
MRS W: Er, thank you.
FRANK: And (6) _____ he?
MRS W: Mr White.
FRANK: Oh!

7 Answer the questions about you.

1 Are you British?

_____

2 Are you 14?

_____

3 Are you clever?

_____

4 Are you tall?

_____

5 Are you busy?

_____

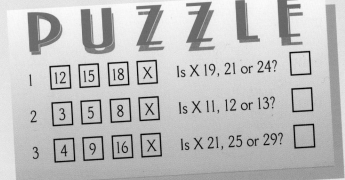

P U Z Z L E

1 | 12 | 15 | 18 | X | Is X 19, 21 or 24? ☐

2 | 3 | 5 | 8 | X | Is X 11, 12 or 13? ☐

3 | 4 | 9 | 16 | X | Is X 21, 25 or 29? ☐

3 A star prize! What is it?

1a Read the advert.

b Find two questions in the advert.

1 _____

2 _____

c Write the answers to the questions.

1 _____

2 _____

d Write the question.

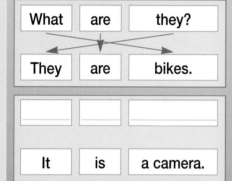

What	are	they?
They	are	bikes.

It	is	a camera.

WIN! WIN! WIN PRIZES!
STAR PRIZE!

What is it?
and 3 BIG PRIZES
What are they?

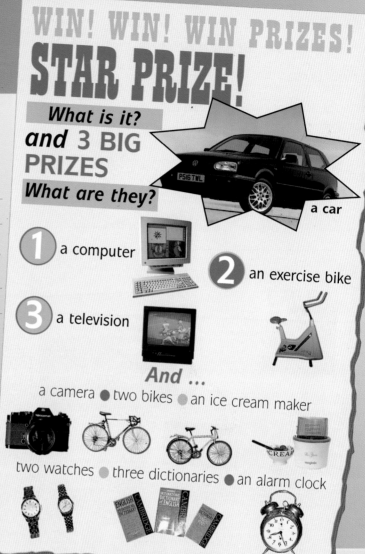

a car

1 a computer

2 an exercise bike

3 a television

And ...

a camera ● two bikes ● an ice cream maker

two watches ● three dictionaries ● an alarm clock

2a Look at the words from the advert.

1	2+ (= plural)
clock	clocks
bike	bikes
watch	watches
dictionary	dictionaries

b Write the plural form of the words.

dish _____

baby _____

bag _____

cake

CHECK THE ANSWERS AND STUDY THE CHARTS ON PAGE 61.

3 Write the plural form of the words below in the chart.

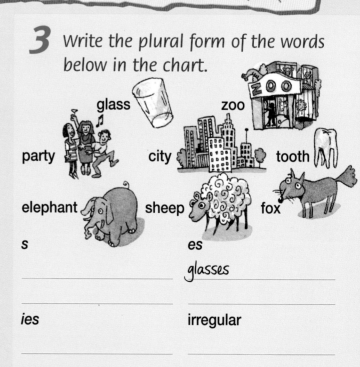

glass   zoo

party   city   tooth

elephant   sheep   fox

s	es
	glasses

ies	irregular

8

4a Read the advert again. Write **a** or **an** with the words below.

_____ camera   _____ exercise bike
_____ television   _____ alarm clock

b Look at the first letters of the words. What is the rule for **a** or **an**?

►► CHECK THE ANSWERS ON PAGE 61.

5 Write sentences with **a** or **an**.

1 It's a glass.
2 _____
3 _____
4 _____
5 _____
6 _____

6 Write questions and answers with **it** or **they**.

1 What are they?
   They're sheep.
2 _____
   _____
3 _____
   _____
4 _____
   _____
5 _____
   _____
6 _____
   _____

7 Look in your school bag. Write a list of things.

Examples:

an exercise book
three pens

_____
_____
_____
_____
_____

P U Z Z L E

Make words. Use blue letters only once in a word. Use red letters (vowels) once or more than once.

b	y	e	g
a	c	m	k
r	t	h	d
w	s	p	i

5+ words = not bad
8+ words = good
10+ words = very good
12+ words = excellent!

4 It's an excellent film!

Films on TV

BATMAN FOREVER!

Actors:
Val Kilmer, Jim Carrey, Nicole Kidman

Batman Forever is an excellent film. The film's exciting and the actors are very good. Jim Carrey is the Joker. He's funny and frightening. Batman Forever is a great adventure!

1a Read **Films on TV**.

b Draw the stars(*).

* = not bad   ** = good
*** = very good   **** = excellent

2a Read **Films on TV** again. Complete the sentences about **Batman Forever**.

	adjective	noun
1 It's an		.
2 It's a		.

b Write the words below in the correct order.

| actors | great | they're |

c Look at the sentences below.

1 It's a film.
   It's **an** excellent film.
2 It's **an** adventure.
   It's **a** great adventure.

d Write **a** or **an**.

1 She's _____ good actor.
2 He's _____ funny man.
3 It's _____ exciting adventure.

e What are the rules?

3 Write sentences with **a** or **an** and the words below.

exciting   expensive   old
short   ~~tall~~   young

1 He's a tall man.

2

3

4

5

6

CHECK THE ANSWERS ON PAGE 62.

4a Look at **Films on TV** again. Complete the sentences below.

Batman Forever is (1) _____ excellent film!
(2) _____ film's exciting.

b Complete the sentences below.

Batman Forever is (1) _____ great adventure.
(2) _____ adventure is exciting.

c What is the rule?

CHECK THE ANSWERS ON PAGE 62.

5 Look at the pictures in exercise 3 again. Write other sentences about the things/people in the pictures with **The**.

1 The man is 2 metres. _____
2 _____
3 _____
4 _____
5 _____
6 _____

6 Look at the answers to the personality test. Write sentences about Sue.

1 She isn't an untidy person.
  She's tidy.
2 _____
3 _____
4 _____
5 _____

personality test

NAME *Sue*

Are you ...?

untidy ☐   ☑ tidy
happy ☑   ☐ sad
serious ☐   ☑ funny
friendly ☑   ☐ unfriendly
lazy ☐   ☑ hardworking

7 Write about you. Use the words from the personality test.

Example:

I'm not a tidy person. I'm untidy.

1 _____
2 _____
3 _____
4 _____
5 _____

PUZZLE

Choose the correct adjective. Draw a picture.

| happy | clever | friendly |

a dangerous dog

a lazy leopard

an angry ant

a _____ cat

11

5 These are my posters

1a Look at the posters.

b Match the posters with the sentences.

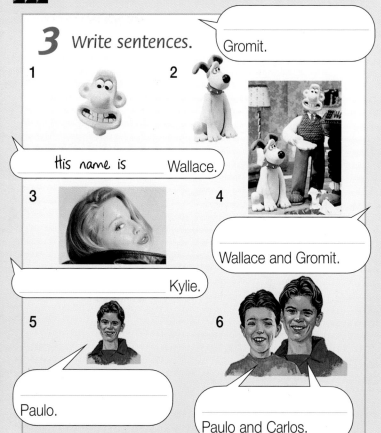

My name's Paulo. These are my posters.

1 This is Wallace. He's an inventor. This is his dog. Its name is Gromit.

2 This is Kylie. She's a singer. Kylie's music is great and her songs are excellent!

3 These are foxes. They're wild dogs. Their home is underground.

2 Look at the sentences in exercise 1 again. Match the words below.

- he
- they
- it
- she
- Kylie
- their
- his
- her
- Kylie's
- its

CHECK THE ANSWERS AND STUDY THE CHARTS ON PAGE 62.

3 Write sentences.

Gromit.

1

2

His name is _____ Wallace.

3

4

_____ Kylie.

Wallace and Gromit.

5

6

Paulo.

Paulo and Carlos.

4 Look at the pictures. Write sentences.

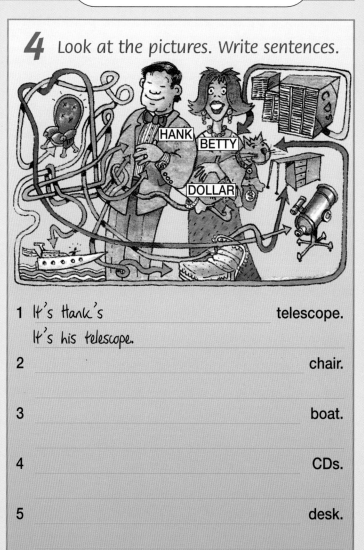

HANK BETTY DOLLAR

1 It's Hank's _____ telescope.
It's his telescope.

2 _____ chair.

3 _____ boat.

4 _____ CDs.

5 _____ desk.

6 _____ bed.

5 Read the farmer's sentences. Complete the chart.

This is my pig. These are my chickens.

That's my horse. Those are my cows.

	near	far	1	2+
this	✓	✗	✓	✗
these				
that				
those				

CHECK YOUR ANSWERS ON PAGE 62.

6 Complete the farmer's sentences.

1

_____ This is _____ my dog.

_____ my sheep.

2

_____ my dog.

_____ my sheep.

3

_____ my dog.

_____ my sheep.

4

_____ my dog.

_____ my sheep.

7 Draw a picture of your bedroom. Draw arrows (→) and write sentences about the things in your bedroom.

1 _____

2 _____

3 _____

4 _____

5 _____

6 _____

7 _____

PUZZLE

This is Tom's mother's only brother's only sister's only child. Who is he?

6 Whose breakfast is this?

1a Read the conversation.

AL: This is my breakfast. Whose burger with chips is this? Is this yours, Babs?

BABS: No, it isn't. It's Dave's. Eggs, beans and chips. That's mine. This is yours, Clare – the burger.

CLARE: No, it isn't. The bacon, egg and toast is mine. So whose breakfast is this?

DAVE: That's mine too.

b Write the person's name with the correct picture.

1 _____   2 _____

3 _____   4 _____

3 Complete the sentences with the words below.

hers   his   mine   ours   theirs   yours

1 This is ___mine___ .

2 Are those _____

No, those are _____ .

3

4 This is _____ .

And this is _____ .

5

6 This is _____ .

2 Match the sentences.

It's my breakfast. •   • It's hers.
It's your breakfast. •   • It's yours.
It's his breakfast. •   • It's mine.
It's her breakfast. •   • It's his.

It's our breakfast. •   • It's theirs.
It's their breakfast. •   • It's the dog's.
It's Dave's breakfast. •   • It's the dogs'.
It's the dog's breakfast. •   • It's ours.
It's the dogs' breakfast. •   • It's Dave's.

 CHECK THE ANSWERS ON PAGE 63.

4a Look at exercise 1. Put the words below in the correct order. Make questions.

1 | breakfast | this | is | Whose | ?

_____

2 | yours | Is | this | ?

_____

b Write the missing words. Make questions.

1 _____ breakfasts _____ those?

2 _____ those yours?

CHECK YOUR ANSWERS ON PAGE 63.

5 Complete the questions and answers. Use **Whose** or **Is** or **Are**, and **this** or **these**.

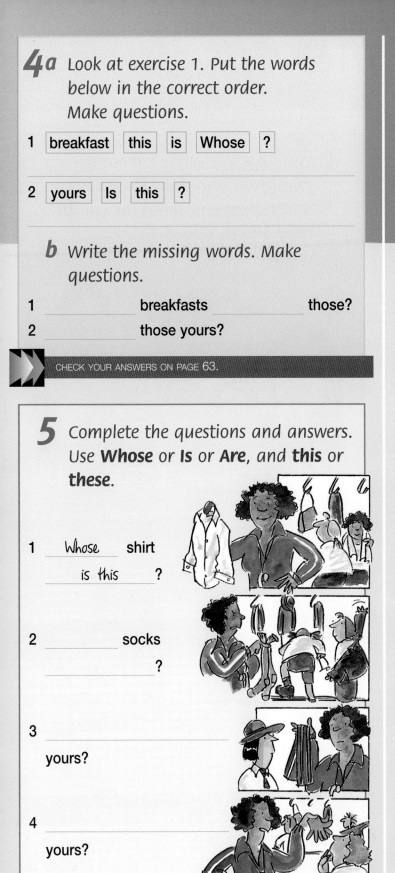

1 _Whose_ shirt
   is this ?

2 _____ socks
   _____ ?

3 _____
   yours?

4 _____
   yours?

5 _____ shoe
   _____ ?

6 Complete the sentences.

1 The telescope is mine and the ball
  ___is___ ___mine___ too.

2 The camera is my mum's and the
  skates _____ _____ too.

3 The cassettes are Mum and Dad's and
  the video _____ _____ too.

4 The books are my dad's and the old
  teddy _____ _____ too!

7 Write sentences about your family and/or friends' things.

Example:

The car is my mum and dad's and the dog is theirs too. The cat is mine!

_____
_____
_____
_____
_____
_____

PUZZLE

Whose fish is it? Draw the lines to the fishing rods.

A: The bag isn't mine.

B: The fish isn't mine.

C: The bike and the fish
   aren't mine.

D: The shoe is mine.

1 Write sentences and questions. Use **Who**/**What** and the words below.

dangerous ~~dirty~~ fast happy ~~old~~

sad short slow strong tall

1

2

3

4 Hello, I'm Bill.

5 I'm Ann.

1 It's old and it's dirty.
   What is it?

2 _____

3 _____

4 _____

5 _____

2 Write answers to the questions in exercise 1.

1 It's a car.

2 _____

3 _____

4 _____

5 _____

3 Write Sue's questions about the puppies (= young dogs) and her dad's questions about the car. Use **they** and **it**. Complete the short answers.

PUPPIES for sale

SPORTS CAR for sale

1 _____ Are they _____ young?
Yes, _____

2 _____ friendly?
Yes, _____

3 _____ beautiful?
Yes, _____

4 _____ clever?
No, _____ !

5 _____ new?
No, it _____

6 _____ red?
No, _____

7 _____ fast?
Yes, _____

8 _____ expensive?
Er, yes, _____ !

4a Match the words and write sentences.

1	expensive •	• boy
2	funny •	• university
3	old •	• bike
4	untidy •	• cat
5	exciting •	• film
6	lazy •	• comic

1 It's an expensive bike.

2 _____

3 _____

4 _____

5 _____

6 _____

b Write sentences with **The**.

1 The bike is expensive.

2 _____

3 _____

4 _____

5 _____

6 _____

5 Complete the chart.

I		my		mine	
you					
		his			
she					
it				~~its~~	
Sue					
the cat					
		our			
				yours	
they					
the cats					

6 Write the teacher's questions and the students' answers. Use **Whose** and **this/that** or **these/those**.

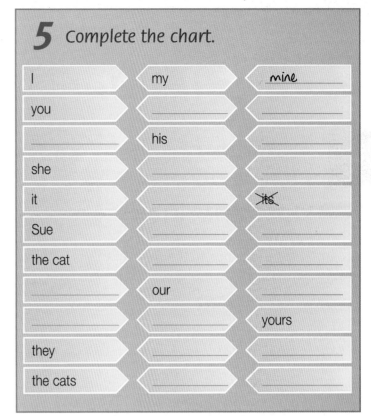

1 Whose mouse is this?

   That's mine.

2

3

17

7 Tina hasn't got a home

1a Read the advert.

b Answer the questions.

1 Is Tina a good dog?

_____

2 Are the things in the picture Tina's? _____

This is Tina.

She's got a great personality –
but she hasn't got a home.

HAVE YOU GOT A HOME FOR TINA?

✂ **DOGS' HOMES UK**

Name: _____

2a Match the words.

I   you
we   they   • has
              • hasn't
              • have
she he it • • haven't

b Put the words in the sentences below in the correct boxes.

She   has   got a home.
She   hasn't got a home.
Has   she   got a home?

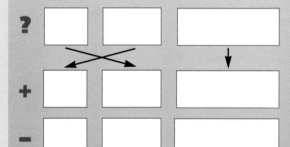

? | | |

+ | | |

– | | |

c Match the questions and answers.

	• Yes, I have.
Have you got a dog? •	• Yes, he has.
Has he got a dog? •	• No, he hasn't.
	• No, I haven't.

---

3 Read the two answers to the dogs' home advert.

✂
Name: _Joe Turner_
Have you got:
① a house / flat / other
② a garden? ✗
   children? ✗
③ pet(s)? _1 cat_

✂
Name: _Mr and Mrs Mill_
Have you got:
④ a house / flat / other
   a garden? ✓
⑤ children? _1 girl_
⑥ pet(s)? _1 mouse_

Write sentences about Joe Turner and Mr and Mrs Mill.

1 _Joe has got a flat._

2 _____

3 _____

4 _____

5 _____

6 _____

CHECK YOUR ANSWERS AND STUDY THE CHARTS ON PAGE 63.

4 Complete the speech bubbles with the words below.

bad tooth   broken leg   headache
sore finger   stomach-ache   toothache

1 I've got a toothache.

2

3

4

5

6

6 Now write answers about you for the questions in exercise 5.

1 Yes, it has./No, it hasn't.

2

3

4

5

7 Have you got the things below? Write sentences.

1 bike   2 broken leg   3 dog   4 good personality
5 husband/wife   6 telescope   7 watch

1 I've got a bike./I haven't got a bike.

2

3

4

5

6

7

5 Look at the graph. It shows childrens' answers to questions about computers.

The Computer Age

100

school

50

you
(at home)

father
(at work)

mother
(at work)

grand-
parents

0

Write the computer company's questions.

1 Has your school got a computer?

2

3

4

5

PUZZLE

Ann and Bill have got five sweets.

Bill and Clare have got four sweets.

Clare and Ann have got three sweets.

Ann has got _____ sweet(s).

Bill has got _____ sweet(s).

Clare has got _____ sweet(s).

Ann, Bill and Clare have got _____ sweets.

19

1a Read the conversation.

MEMORY TEST

Speech bubbles:
- There's a pen. There are some keys. Er ...
- Is there a dictionary?
- Yes, there is.
- Is there an alarm clock?
- Yes, er – Sorry. There isn't an alarm clock.
- Are there any comics?
- No, there aren't. There aren't any comics but there is a book.

b Look at the girl's answers again. Is she right (✓) or wrong (✗)?

a Yes, there is. ☐

b There isn't an alarm clock. ☐

c No, there aren't. ☐

2 Read the conversation again. Write **a/an**, **some** and **any** in the chart below.

	+	–	?
singular (1)	a/an		
plural (2+)			

3 Complete the charts.

	is	bag.
	isn't	orange.
____	are	comics.
	aren't	CDs.

Is	____	bag?
		apple?
Are	____	watches?

Yes,		____ .
		____ .
No,		____ .
		____ .

CHECK THE ANSWERS AND STUDY THE CHARTS ON PAGE 64.

4 Complete the sentences about the cupboard. Use **There is/There are** or **There isn't/aren't**.

Labels: radio, cassettes, magazines, axe, box, newspapers

1 There is a _____ box.

2 _____ ball.

3 _____ bike.

4 _____ books.

5 _____ axe.

6 _____ cassettes.

7 _____ magazines.

8 _____ skates.

5 Look at the Holiday Hotel. Write sentences about it with **There is** or **There are**.

HOLIDAY H·O·T·E·L

1 Swimming pool
2 Telephones
3 Car park
4 Shops
5 Restaurant
6 Garden
7 Lifts

1 There is a swimming pool.
2
3
4
5
6
7

6a Ask questions about Sun Hotel. Use the words in exercise 5.

1 Is there a swimming pool?
2
3
4
5
6
7

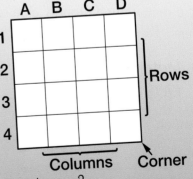

b Look at the information. Answer the questions.

1 No, there isn't.
2
3
4
5
6
7

7 Write about the things in your bedroom. Use **There is/are** or **There isn't/aren't**.

Examples:

There are some books./There aren't any books.

1
2
3
4
5
6
7

P U Z Z L E

Look at the picture. There are four black squares. The other squares are white. Read the sentences and colour the correct squares black.

	A	B	C	D
1				
2				
3				
4				

Rows

Columns   Corner

There are two black squares in row 2.
The corner squares aren't black.
There are two black squares in column C.
There are two black squares in row 4.
There is one black square in column A.

9 How much orange juice is there?

1a Read the conversation.

How many oranges are there?

Four.

I've got thirty.

Hello, Paulo. How many oranges have you got?

How much sugar is there?

Fifty grams.

I'm hungry. Are there any crisps or sandwiches?

No, but there are some oranges – and there is some orange juice now.

b Answer the questions.

1 How much sugar is there? _50 grams_

2 How much orange juice is there? _____

3 How many oranges are there? _34_

4 How many glasses are there? _____

2a Choose the correct words in the sentences below.

1 There is/are some oranges.

2 How many/much oranges is/are there?

3 There is/are some orange juice.

4 How many/much orange juice is/are there?

b Match the words with the pictures.

much   many

•   •

•   •   •

3 Put the things below in the correct list.

banana   burger   cake   cereal

coffee   egg   lemonade   meat

oil   sandwich   sausage   water

ORANGES	SUGAR *NOT* SUGARS
apples	bacon
biscuits	chicken
chips	fruit
crisps	tea

CHECK YOUR ANSWERS AND STUDY THE INFORMATION ON PAGE 64.

4 Write sentences with **There is some** or **There are some**.

1 _____

2 There is some chicken.

3 _____

4 _____

5 _____

6 _____

7 _____

8 _____

5 Write questions about the things in exercise 4. Use **How much** or **How many**.

1 _____

2 How much chicken is there?

3 _____

4 _____

5 _____

6 _____

7 _____

8 _____

6 Complete the conversation with the words below.

~~any~~   are   are   is   isn't   many
much   some   there

Is there (1) _____any_____ soap?

Yes, (2) _____ is.

How (3) _____ shampoo is there?

We've got (4) _____ shampoo too.

Yes, but how (5) _____ bottles of shampoo (6) _____ there?

There (7) _____ two.

And (8) _____ there any toothpaste?

No, there (9) _____ .

7 Write about the things in your bathroom. Use **There is** and **There are**.

1 _____

2 _____

3 _____

4 _____

5 _____

P U Z Z L E

A mother and a father have got three daughters. Each daughter has got two brothers. How many children are there?

_____

1a Read about Sue's kitchen.

Sue's mum is angry. There is orange juice and water on the kitchen floor. The dirty spoons are on the fridge. The dirty jug is in the sink. The dishes are under the table. There's an orange behind the door, the sugar bag is next to the bin and there's an orange between the cooker and the fridge ...

Sue! Where are you?

b Complete the answers to the questions about the kitchen. Use **in**, **on** or **under**.

1 Where's the plate?   It's _____in_____ the sink.

2 Where's the knife?   It's _____ the table.

3 Where are the dirty glasses?
   They're _____ the table.

2 Write the correct words for the pictures.

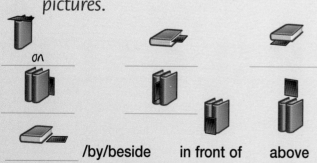

on

/by/beside   in front of   above

CHECK YOUR ANSWERS ON PAGE 65.

3 Write questions with **Where is ... ?** or **Where are ... ?**

1 Where is the dog?

It's under the TV.

2 _____

It's in the bin.

3 _____

They're by the telephone.

4 _____

It's above the cooker.

5 _____

They're between the magazines and the newspapers.

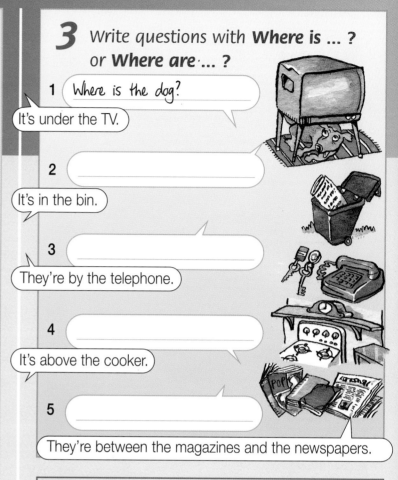

4 Look at the picture and complete the sentences.

1 The post office is _____ the river.
2 The postbox is _____ the bridge.
3 The café is _____ the park.
4 The bookshop is _____ the bank and the newsagent.
5 The bus stop is _____ the bank.

5 Look at the fridge. Write sentences. Use **There** and the words below.

above   behind   between
in front of   ~~next to~~   under

1 _There is a fish next to_ some lemonade.

2 _____
_____ a fish and some orange juice.

3 _____
_____ some sausages.

4 _____
_____ some eggs.

5 _____
_____ some chicken.

6 _____
_____ some meat.

6 Where are the things now? Write sentences with **The**.

1 The fish is between the lemonade and the orange juice.

2 _____
_____ fish.

3 _____
_____ sausages.

4 _____
_____ ice cream.

5 _____
_____ chicken.

6 _____
_____ eggs.

7 What's in your fridge? Write six sentences.

1 _____
2 _____
3 _____
4 _____
5 _____
6 _____

PUZZLE

There are some ducks on a river. There are two ducks in front of a duck, two ducks behind a duck and one duck between the ducks. How many ducks are there?

_____

11 Don't sit in the sun

Happy Holidays ...

1 Wear sunglasses and a hat.

2 Don't sit in the sun at midday.

3 Use sun cream.

4 Don't use oil.

5 Drink water, fruit juice or other cold drinks. (Try Cool Caribbean Carrot Juice.)

1a Read **Happy Holidays**.

b Are the things below good(✓) or bad(✗)?

1 sunglasses and a hat ☐

2 sun at midday ☐

3 sun cream ☐

4 oil ☐

5 water and fruit juice ☐

c One word in **Happy Holidays** = no.
What is it? _____

---

2 Finish the sentences below about **Happy Holidays**.

1 _____ lemonade.

2 _____ stand in the sun at midday.

 CHECK YOUR ANSWERS ON PAGE 65.

---

3 Read the recipe for Cool Caribbean Carrot Juice. The sentences are in the wrong order. Match them with the pictures.

a Add the lemon juice to the jug. ☐

b Finally, add ice and stir. ☐

c Next, squeeze one lemon. ☐

d First, put two glasses of carrot juice and one glass of pineapple juice in a jug. ☐ 1

e Then pour the juice into small glasses. ☐

Happy Holidays ... **Cool Caribbean Carrot Juice**

---

4 Write sentences for the signs and pictures. Use the words below.

drink the water   wash your hands
drop litter   ~~take photos~~   turn left
turn right   walk on the grass

1   2   3

4   5   6

7

1 Don't take photos.

2 _____

3 _____

4 _____

5 _____

6 _____

7 _____

26

5 Complete the school rules. Use the words below.

be do̶ eat listen play run sit wear

——— RULES ———

Dos …
- ❶ ___Do___ your homework.
- ❷ _____ your school uniform.
- ❸ _____ to your teacher.
- ❹ _____ good!

Don'ts …
- ❶ _____ sweets in the classroom.
- ❷ _____ computer games in the classroom.
- ❸ _____ on the desks.
- ❹ _____ in the classroom.

6 Write the teacher's sentences.

put run stand use wash̶

1 Wash your hands.

7 What are your school rules? Write a list.

Example:

Do your homework.

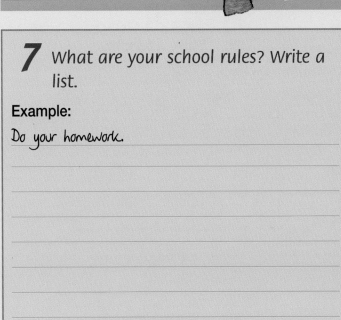

PUZZLE

Use twelve pens and make this pattern.
Move only two pens and make seven squares.

27

What can you do?

1a Read the text.

Newborn babies can taste and smell but they can't see clearly. They cannot focus their eyes.

A baby gorilla can focus at about two weeks. It can crawl at nine weeks and it can walk on two legs at about nine months.

What can we do? Babies can focus at about six months, they can crawl at nine months and they can walk at about one year.

At one year, babies can also say one or two words and they can understand words. What about gorillas? Can they understand words?

Gorilla

| WEEKS | 1 | ② | 3 | 4 | 5 | 6 | 7 | 8 | ⑨ |
| MONTHS | 1 | 2 | 3 | 4 | 5 | ⑥ | 7 | 8 | ⑨ 10 11 ⑫ |

Mama!

Baby

b What can they do? Tick (✓) or cross (✗).

1 At ten months, a baby can crawl. ☐

2 At seven months, a baby can walk. ☐

3 At ten months, a gorilla can walk. ☐

c Tick the correct answer about babies at nine months.

Can they crawl?   Yes, they can. ☐
                  No, they can't. ☐

2 Complete the sentences about babies at nine months.

_____ _____ they do?

They _____ crawl. They _____
walk.

_____ they run?

No, they _____ .

3 What can children and gorillas do at ten years? Write sentences with the words below.

    1 read   2 write   3 climb trees
        4 run   5 use a telephone

1 Children can read.
  Gorillas can't read.

2 _____

3 _____

4 _____

5 _____

CHECK YOUR ANSWERS AND STUDY THE CHARTS ON PAGE 65.

4 Ask questions about the people in the pictures with these words.

dance   play tennis   ride a bike   sing
~~speak Chinese~~   swim

您 早
好 安
??

1 Can he speak Chinese?
2 _____
3 _____
4 _____
5 _____
6 _____

5 Write short answers to the questions in exercise 4.

1 No, he can't.
2 _____
3 _____
4 _____
5 _____
6 _____

6 Complete the conversation.

_____ _____ you
_____ see _____? _____
you _____ Saturn?

No, I _____. I _____
_____ Saturn. I _____
_____ the back of your head!

7 Write sentences about you. Use **can** or **can't** and the words below.

1 ride   2 speak   3 play   4 dance
5 sing   6 use

1 _____
2 _____
3 _____
4 _____
5 _____
6 _____

PUZZLE

What can you see? Can you see two things in each picture?

1a Write questions. Use **Have ... got**.

1 Have you got any books in your bag?

2 _____

3 _____

4 _____

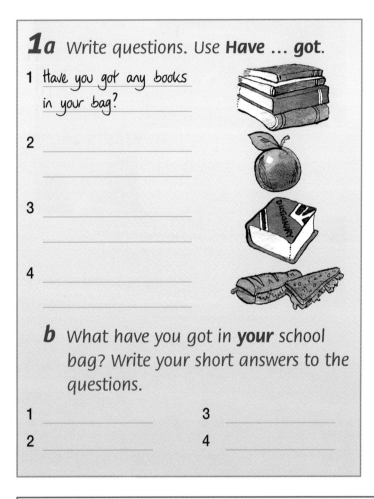

b What have you got in **your** school bag? Write your short answers to the questions.

1 _____   3 _____
2 _____   4 _____

2 Pam is new in town. Complete her questions. Use **there**.

1 _____ Are there any _____ parks?
2 _____ post office?
3 _____ shops?
4 _____ swimming pool?
5 _____ bank?
6 _____ restaurants?

Now look at the map and write the answers.

1 _____
2 _____
3 _____
4 _____
5 _____
6 _____

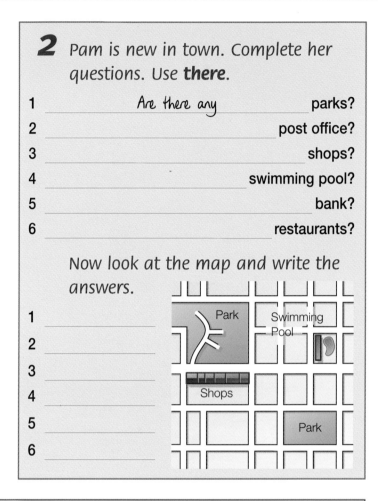

3 The food in the picture is for a party. Sue's mum and dad are busy in the kitchen. Look at Sue's answers and write their questions. Use **How much** or **How many**.

1 How much lemonade is there?
   Three bottles.

2 _____
   Two big dishes.

3 _____
   One plate.

4 _____
   Twenty.

5 _____
   About thirty.

6 _____
   Three.

7 _____
   Two jugs.

4 Look at the picture in exercise 3 again. Complete the questions from the people at the party and write the answers. Use the words below.

1 in front of   2 next to   3 between
4 on   5 in front of   6 behind

1 _____Where's_____ the orange juice?
It's in front of the lemonade.

2 _____ the glasses?
_____

3 _____ the chicken?
_____

4 _____ the sandwiches?
_____ small table.

5 _____ the sausages?
_____

6 _____ the lemonade?
_____

5 Complete the woman's instructions to her son. Use the verbs below.

~~climb~~   eat   read   sit   wash

1 ____Don't climb____ the tree.

2 _____ it!

3 _____ your hands.

4 _____ your book.

5 _____ on the cat!

6 Ask questions about the people in the pictures. Use **can**. Then write short answers.

computer games

1 _Can she swim?_ ? _Yes, she can._

2 _____ ? _____

3 _____ ? _____

4 _____ ? _____

5 _____ ? _____

6 _____ ? _____

31

1a Read about everyday life in Papua New Guinea.

b Match the sentences and the pictures. Are the sentences right (✓) or wrong (✗)?

A   B   C

☐   ☐   1

1 Papuans live in big cities. ☒

2 They paint their faces. ☐

3 They don't eat fruit. ☐

Papua New Guinea

Papua New Guinea is in the Pacific. It has got beautiful mountains and forests, and there are 700 languages.

Papuans live in villages. They keep pigs and chickens and they grow vegetables. They eat bananas and coconuts too. On special days, Papuans paint their faces and wear necklaces of pigs' teeth.

Papuans hunt and fish. They make stone axes. Girls and boys learn from their parents. Some children don't go to school. They live in the mountains and there aren't any roads or schools.

2a Look at the text again. Complete the sentences below.

\+ They ⬚⬚⬚ in villages.

– They ⬚⬚⬚ ⬚⬚⬚ in cities.

b Put the words below in the correct order. Make sentences.

\+ | necklaces | They | wear |

_____

– | wear | don't | school uniforms | They |

_____

CHECK YOUR ANSWERS AND STUDY THE CHART ON PAGE 66.

3 Put the words in the correct order. Make sentences about people around the world.

1 hamburgers don't Papuans eat

Papuans don't eat hamburgers.

2 like Americans baseball

3 Canadians grow don't bananas

4 Italians pizzas eat

5 coffee Brazilians grow

6 don't Italian Papuans speak

4 Complete the sentences about people around the world with the verbs below. Use three negative forms.

drink drive ~~eat~~ go listen live ride

1 Some British children ____eat____ toast and cereal and _____ milk for breakfast.

2 In Australia, some children _____ to school. They _____ to their teacher on the radio.

3 Mongols _____ in houses. They _____ in tents.

4 The Tuareg _____ in the Sahara desert. They _____ cars. They _____ camels.

5 The sentences below are false. Write true sentences.

1 Mosquitoes eat chips. (drink blood)
Mosquitoes don't eat chips.
They drink blood.

2 Cowboys drive buses. (ride horses)
_____
_____

3 Fish fly in the sky. (swim in the sea)
_____
_____

4 You speak a Papuan language.
_____
_____

6 Match the words.

1 collect •   • comics
2 make •   • football
3 play •   • models
4 read •   • a motorbike
5 ride •   • stamps
6 watch •   • TV

7 Use the words in exercise 6 and write true sentences about you.

Examples: I collect stamps./I don't collect stamps.

1 _____
2 _____
3 _____
4 _____
5 _____
6 _____

PUZZLE

Match the friends with their hobbies.

I don't collect stamps.

Babs and I don't play a musical instrument.

I don't make models.

I don't play the guitar.

33

14 Do you play the drums?

1a Read the conversation.

PAULO: Do you play the piano, Kim?
KIM: No, I don't. I play the drums. I practise every day.
PAULO: Where do you play?
KIM: In my bedroom. I've got a big drum kit.
PAULO: When do you practise?
KIM: I get up at six o'clock and practise. Then I have breakfast and go to school.
PAULO: Six o'clock! What do your neighbours think?
KIM: Oh, they like the drums.
PAULO: How do you know?
KIM: They play too. They use the walls.
PAULO: Oh!

b Put the pictures in the correct order. Write 1, 2 and 3 in the boxes.

☐ ☐ ☐

3 Use the words below and make questions with Do.

~~a car~~   English   homework   the piano
the radio   songs

1 _Do you_   drive   _a car?_
2 _____   listen to   _____
3 _____   study   _____
4 _____   do   _____
5 _____   sing   _____
6 _____   play   _____

2a Look at Paulo's questions with Where, When, How and Kim's answers again. Now match the questions with the answers below.

1 Do you go to school?   •   • I walk to school.
2 Where do you go to school? •   • I go to school in London.
3 When do you go to school? •   • I study science.
4 How do you go to school?   •   • I go to school in the morning.
5 What do you do at school? •   • Yes, I do.

b Finish the sentences below. Use the conversation for help.

1 _____ you get up at 7.00?

No, I _____ .

2 _____ you get up?

I _____ at 6.00.

4 Write short answers about you to the questions in exercise 3.

1 _____
2 _____
3 _____
4 _____
5 _____
6 _____

 CHECK YOUR ANSWERS AND STUDY THE CHARTS ON PAGE 66.

5a Look at exercises 1 and 2 again. Match the words with the times.

- in
- on
- at
- 1.00/2.00
- the morning
- Monday

CHECK YOUR ANSWERS AND STUDY THE CHARTS ON PAGE 67.

b Complete Kim's letter to her Greek penfriend.

Dear Rula

My new school is great but it's far away. I get up (1) ___at___ 6.00. We start (2) _____ 9.00 and go home (3) _____ 4.00. There's one hour for lunch. I don't like the food – it's terrible!

It's winter now. England is very cold (4) _____ winter. My friends come to my house (5) _____ the evening or I go to theirs. (6) _____ the weekend, we go to the swimming pool. (7) _____ Sunday, I see my grandparents.

Life is different (8) _____ summer! We have six weeks (9) _____ July and August with no school. Can I come to your country for my holiday? Can you come to England?

Love,

Kim

6 Lisa is an American student. Read some British school-children's answers to Lisa's questions. Write her questions.

Do   Do   How   What   When   When   ~~Where~~

1 Where do you go to school?
2 _____
3 _____
4 _____
5 _____
6 _____
7 _____

1 We go to school in Liverpool.
2 We start class at 9 in the morning.
3 We walk to school or go by bus.
4 We study French, history, maths and English.
5 Yes, we do. We have tests.
6 We do our homework in the evening.
7 No, we don't. We don't like homework.

7 Write your answers to the questions in exercise 6.

1 _____
2 _____
3 _____
4 _____
5 _____
6 _____
7 _____

PUZZLE

Babs and her brother:

make models on Monday.
tidy their bedrooms on Tuesday.
watch TV on Wednesday.
take the dog for a walk on Thursday.
fly their model aeroplane on Friday.
see their uncle on Saturday.

What do they do on Sunday?

do their homework ☐   practise the piano ☐

read comics ☐   sing songs ☐

35

15 Sometimes he doesn't wake up for school

1a Read about Chris.

I help at home.

CHRIS HERBERT is 10 years old. His mother is very ill so he always helps at home. He goes to the shops and carries the shopping home. His brothers never help – they can't. Barry is only a baby and Jamie is very ill, too. Chris takes care of his brothers. He cooks the food and washes the dishes. The work is hard and sometimes he doesn't wake up for school.

b Look at these sentences.

I help at home.

Chris helps at home.

c Finish the sentences.

1   I take care of the baby.

Chris _____ care of the baby.

2   I don't wake up for school.

Chris _____ wake up for school.

2a Look at these words from the magazine article about Chris.

I cook	he cooks
I wash	he washes
I carry	he carries
I go	he goes

b Complete the chart.

I watch	he _____
I tidy	he _____
I read	he _____
I do	he _____

3 Kim does some things but doesn't do other things. Write sentences about her.

1 eat   2 read   3 study   4 watch

1 She doesn't eat vegetables. She eats burgers.

2 _____

3 _____

4 _____

CHECK YOUR ANSWERS ON PAGE 67.

4 Write questions about Kim and give short answers.

1 eat burgers   2 read comics
3 study Chinese   4 watch football

1 *Does she eat burgers?*
Yes, she does.

2 _____

_____

3 _____

_____

4 _____

_____

5 Look at the article about Chris Herbert again. Find the words **always**, **never**, **sometimes**. Put them in the diagram below.

	often	rarely	

_____   often   rarely

100% ◄──────────────────────────────► 0%

            usually   _____   _____

CHECK YOUR ANSWERS ON PAGE 67.

How many days a week do you do these things?								
	0	1	2	3	4	5	6	7
go to the cinema			✓					
meet your friends					✓			
go jogging	✓							
tidy your bedroom		✓						
listen to the radio							✓	
brush your teeth								✓

6 Look at the information about Kim. Write sentences about her. Use the words in exercise 5.

1 *She sometimes goes to the cinema.*

2 _____

3 _____

4 _____

5 _____

6 _____

7 Write sentences about your friend for the things in exercise 6.

1 _____

2 _____

3 _____

4 _____

5 _____

6 _____

PUZZLE

Joanne drives her car to work in the morning. The journey takes 80 minutes. The same journey in her husband's car takes one hour and 20 minutes. Explain.

16 She hates speaking English

1a Read about Paulo.

Paulo's mother is Brazilian but she lives in England. Brazil is a beautiful country and she often thinks about it.

Paulo's grandmother lives in Rio and Paulo and his parents sometimes visit her. They usually go in February for the carnival. Paulo's grandmother is very old so she can't visit them, but she loves Paulo and always telephones him on Sunday. She talks to him in Portuguese. She hates speaking English!

Paulo loves Brazil. He loves the music and enjoys singing and dancing. He likes swimming in the sea and lying on a hot beach.

b Are these sentences right or wrong?

1 Paulo never visits his grandmother. ☐
2 She can't visit Paulo and his family. ☐
3 Paulo's grandmother likes English. ☐
4 Paulo can swim. ☐
5 He can't dance. ☐

2a Read Paulo's sentence.

> I love my grandmother and she loves me.

b Find **it**, **her**, **him** and **them** in the article. Write the words in the chart.

I	me	we	us
you	you	you	you
she			
he		they	
it			

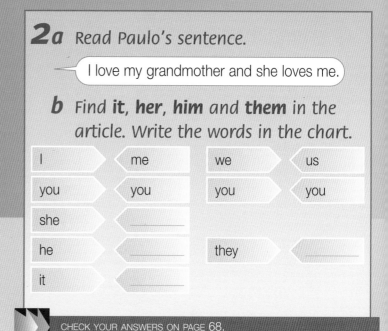

CHECK YOUR ANSWERS ON PAGE 68.

3 Write **me**, **you**, **him**, **her**, **it**, **us** or **them**.

1 Where are my shoes? Can you see _them_ ?

2 Can you help _____ ?

3 You're terrible! I hate _____ !

4 Your mother understands maths. Ask _____.

5 Your hands are dirty. Wash _____.

6 I want _____. Give it to _____.

4a Look at the -ing forms. Write the verbs.

dancing _____   swimming _____

lying _____   singing _____

b How do you make the -ing form of verbs?

Example: dance – ~~e~~ + -ing = dancing

c Write the -ing form of the verbs below.

speak	speaking	wash	_____
take	_____	make	_____
die	_____	tie	_____
run	_____	put	_____

▶▶▶ CHECK YOUR ANSWERS ON PAGE 68.

5 We often use -ing words with enjoy, like, love, hate.

Write sentences with the words below.

eat   ~~get up~~   lie   shop   walk   use

1 He hates getting up. _____
2 _____
3 _____
4 _____
5 _____
6 _____

6 Complete Paulo's letter to his grandmother. Use you, her, them, us, me and the -ing form of write, read, study.

Dear Grandma,

Thank you for the Brazilian cassettes. I listen to
(1) ___them___ every day.

There's a new music teacher at school. She's great. We
like (2) _____ . We enjoy (3) _____ music in her
class. I usually hate (4) _____ projects at school,
but we've got a project about world music. Can you give
(5) _____ any information about music in South
America?

We enjoy (6) _____ your letters. Please write to (7)
_____ soon. We often think about (8) _____

Love,

Paulo

7 Look at exercise 5 again. Do you enjoy/like/love/hate these things? Write sentences.

1 _____
2 _____
3 _____
4 _____
5 _____
6 _____

PUZZLE

The mad professor hates washing but loves cleaning.
He hates walking but loves dancing.
He hates sitting but loves standing.
He hates asking but loves answering.
Explain.

39

1a Read about the football match.

These men usually win but they aren't winning today. They're playing a very slow game.

Are they feeling tired?

The people in the stadium are standing up and shouting. And Ronaldo's got the ball ... He's running past one man, two men ...

and it's a goal!

b Match the pictures with the sentences.

A   B

C   D

1 They're standing up and shouting. ☐

2 He's running past one man. ☐

3 It's a goal! ☐

4 They're playing football. ☐

2 Look at exercise 1 again. Complete the questions and answers.

1 ___Are___ they playing basketball?

No, they aren't. They're _____ football.

2 ___Is___ the woman watching TV?

No, she _____ . _____ to the radio.

3 _____ the people shouting?

Yes, they _____ .

CHECK YOUR ANSWERS AND STUDY THE CHARTS ON PAGE 68.

3 Write affirmative or negative sentences. Use the verbs below.

do   eat   paint   sit   walk   wear

1 I'm painting a picture.

2 on my coat.

3 your school uniform.

4 Look! _____ .

5 your homework.

6 their dinner.

4 The teacher is late. Write about the students.

1 She's dancing.
2 _____ on the board.
3 _____
4 _____
5 _____

5 Write the teacher's questions and the students' answers. Use the words in exercise 4.

1 Are you dancing?
  No, I'm not. I'm tidying the books.
2 _____
  _____
3 _____
4 _____
5 _____

6 Where's James? Use the words below and complete the telephone conversation.

be   carry   not listen   ride   telephone   wear

Hello, police?

Yes, I _____ (1) about my son. He's very late home.

Yes, he _____ (2) a blue bike. His clothes? He _____ (3) jeans and a red shirt. And he _____ (4) a red bag.

His hair? It's black, and it _____ (5) long. I don't like it but – Oh, wait a minute, the door – JAMES! WHAT'S THAT? IT'S DIRTY – TAKE IT AWAY! JAMES, YOU _____ (6) TO ME! JAMES! I – Oh, I'm sorry, Officer. It's him. Goodbye.

7 Write short answers to the questions about you.

1 Are you playing football?

_____

2 Are you sitting in the kitchen?

_____

3 Are you wearing jeans?

_____

4 Are you listening to the radio?

_____

5 Are you feeling tired?

_____

PUZZLE

There are 670 students at school. 7% are carrying one book. Half of the other 93% are carrying two books, and half are not carrying any books.

How many books are there?
(This is easy. Don't use maths!)

18 What is James doing?

ECLIPSE OF THE MOON

1a Read about James.

It's 2 a.m. James is sitting in his bedroom. He usually goes to bed at about 10.30 but tonight he's staying up late.

He studies the planets and looks at the sky every night. Tonight he is looking at the moon. He's waiting for an eclipse.

b Complete the sentences.

1 James _____ at the sky every night.

2 He _____ at the moon now.

c Match the verbs from the sentences above with the diagrams below.

past   now   future   past   now   future

_____   _____

2a Put the words below in the correct order to make questions.

1 | doing | is | James | What | ? |

_____

2 | James | Where | sitting | is | ? |

_____

b Read about James again and answer the questions.

1 _____

2 _____

CHECK YOUR ANSWERS ON PAGE 69.

3 Complete the chart with the correct forms of the verb **study**.

present simple		present continuous
I	study	I'm studying
you		
she		
he		
it		
we		
they		

4 The next day, James is in his science class. Complete the text with the correct form of the verbs below.

1 like   2 not listen   3 think   4 know
5 watch   6 know   7 know   8 sleep

James _____ likes _____ (1) science but today he _____ (2). He _____ (3) about last night. The teacher _____ (4) James has got a telescope. He's got one too and he _____ (5) the stars. He _____ (6) about James's late night. How _____ he _____ (7) ? James _____ (8)!

5 Kim is having a barbecue. Complete her conversation with James. Use **What**, **Where** and the verbs in the box.

JAMES: _____ you _____ (1)?

KIM: I _____ (2).

JAMES: _____ you _____ (3)?

KIM: Sausages and chicken. _____ you _____ (4)?

JAMES: Sausages, please. Have you got any music? _____ (5) your cassettes?

KIM: In the cupboard. Here they are. _____ you _____ (6)?

JAMES: The sausages are on fire!

6 Write questions and answers.

1

What are you doing?

_____

What do you do?

I'm a dentist.

2

_____

_____

_____

_____

3

_____

_____

_____

_____

7 Write answers to the questions about you.

1 What are you reading?

_____

2 What do you read at the weekend?

_____

3 What does your father do?

_____

4 What is your mother doing?

_____

5 Do you eat ice cream?

_____

6 Are you eating ice cream?

_____

PUZZLE

A man is looking at a photo.

I haven't got any brothers or sisters but this man's father is my father's son.

Who is he looking at in the photo?

1 Look at Sue's school timetable. Write sentences. Use **eat**, **play**, **study** and **at**, **in**, **on**.

1 She _____ French _____ Tuesday.

2 She _____ lunch _____ the afternoon.

3 She _____ science _____ Monday _____ 1.00.

4 She _____ tennis _____ Monday _____ the morning.

5 She _____ maths _____ 9.30 _____ Monday morning.

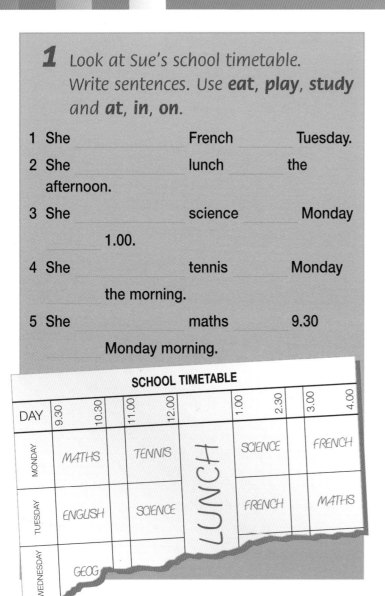

DAY	9.30	10.30	11.00	12.00	1.00	2.30	3.00	4.00
MONDAY	MATHS		TENNIS		LUNCH	SCIENCE		FRENCH
TUESDAY	ENGLISH		SCIENCE			FRENCH		MATHS
WEDNESDAY	GEOG							

SCHOOL TIMETABLE

2 Look at the 'Axe Man' and 'Crazy Cat' computer games results after ten games. Write sentences about the players. Use the verb **win** and **always**, **usually**, **often**, **sometimes**, **rarely**, **never**.

AXE MAN		CRAZY CAT	
JAMES	10	KIM	10
SUE	9	PAULO	9
ERIC	7	SUE	8
KIM	2	JAMES	3
PAULO	1	ERIC	0

1 James _always wins_ at Axe Man.

2 Kim and Paulo _____ at Axe Man.

3 Eric _____ at Axe Man.

4 Paulo and Sue _____ at Crazy Cat.

5 James _____ at Crazy Cat.

6 Eric _____ at Crazy Cat.

3 Complete the questions and match the questions with the answers. Use the words below.

How   What   When   When   Where   Where   buy   eat   get up   learn   live   sleep

1 _When do_ we _sleep_ ?   • • At a newsagent.

2 _____ we _____ magazines?   • • At night.

3 _____ English people _____ for breakfast? • • Bacon and eggs, toast or cereal.

4 _____ we _____ new words?   • • In Africa.

5 _____ gorillas _____ ?   • • In the morning.

6 _____ we _____ ?   • • We use a dictionary.

4 Complete the table.

I	my	mine	me
you			
she			
he			
it		~~its~~	
Kim			Kim
the cat			the cat
we		ours	
they	their		
the cats			the cats

1
2

5 Write true sentences. Use (not) like, love, enjoy, hate and the verbs below.

eat go play sit speak
study tidy wash watch

1 I _____ football.

2 I _____ sweets.

3 My friend _____
maths.

4 My mother _____
the dishes.

5 I _____ my
bedroom.

6 My teacher _____
English.

7 I _____ in the sun.

8 My grandparents
_____ TV.

9 My father _____ to
work.

6 Write question and answers. Use What and the present continuous.

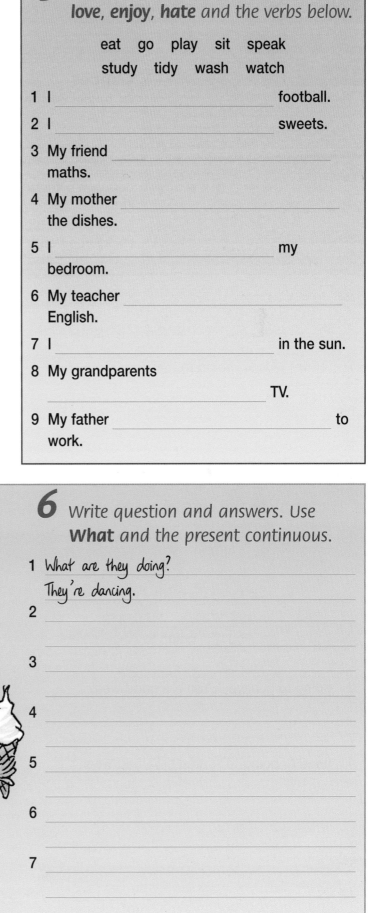

1 What are they doing?
They're dancing.

2 _____

3 _____

4 _____

5 _____

6 _____

7 _____

19 You're going to be busy!

1a Read the texts from a magazine.

b Are the texts talking about the past, present or future?

YOUR STARS NEXT WEEK

Cancer 22 June – 23 July	Aquarius 21 January – 19 February
You're usually shy and you don't meet many people. But next weekend a new and interesting person is going to come into your life. Lucky colour: blue Lucky number: 5 Lucky day: Saturday	Next week you're going to be busy at home and at school. You aren't going to have any free time. You're going to be tired, so don't go to bed late! Lucky colour: green Lucky number: 7 Lucky day: Tuesday

2a Read the texts again. Put the words below in the correct order.

1 [come] [is] [going to]

_____

2 [going to] [have] [aren't]

_____

b Make sentences. Put the words below in the correct order.

1 [aren't] [You] [any free time] [have] [going to]

_____

2 [You're] [be] [busy] [going to]

_____

3 [going to] [have] [You] [a good week] [are]

_____

4 [have] [going to] [aren't] [a bad week] [You]

_____

► CHECK YOUR ANSWERS AND STUDY THE CHARTS ON PAGE 69.

3 Write sentences about Paulo and his family. Use the words below.

1 open/window   2 jump on/table   3 kick/cat
4 eat/chocolates   5 answer/phone   6 go out

1 Paulo's dad is going to open the window.

2 _____

3 _____

4 _____

5 _____

6 _____

46

4 Write sentences. Use **going to** and the words below.

1 throw/ball 2 catch/ball 3 drop/plates 4 break 5 fall in/river

1 She's going to throw the ball.

2 _____

3 _____

4 _____

5 _____

5 Read each sentence and write a second sentence. Use **not going to** and the words below.

1 They don't like parties.   (come)

They aren't going to come.

2 His bike is broken.   (ride)

_____

3 He's tired.   (get up)

_____

4 She hates sausages.   (eat)

_____

5 They are lazy.   (do/homework)

_____

7 Write about your plans for this weekend. Use the words below.

1 watch TV   2 play computer games
3 wash your hair   4 do your homework
5 go to the dentist   6 meet friends

Examples:

I'm going to watch TV./I'm not going to watch TV.

1 _____

2 _____

3 _____

4 _____

5 _____

6 _____

6 Read Paulo's weekend list. Write sentences about him.

1 He's going to wash his dog on Saturday.

2 _____

3 _____

4 _____

5 _____

Saturday
wash dog
take bike to bike shop

Sunday
write to grandma
meet Sue
do music project

PUZZLE

My mother's husband's son is going to have a party next week.

Is this boy going to go to the party?

20 What are you going to watch?

1a Read the conversation.

SUE: What are you going to watch tonight?

ERIC: *Nature Watch.* I always watch it. I love animals.

SUE: Are you going to stay up for the horror film?

ERIC: Yes, I am. Are you going to watch it?

SUE: At 12.00! No, I'm not. It's late. What are you going to watch on Sunday?

ERIC: Look. I'm going to watch these programmes …

b Look at the TV page. Eric is going to watch two programmes on Saturday. Tick (✓) them.

Television this weekend

Saturday

8.00 pm	**Music hour**
9.00 pm	**Nature Watch –** *The life of elephants in Africa*
10.00 pm	**Guns for Dollars –** *Cowboy adventure*
12.00 am	**The Thing 3 –** *A frightening horror story*

Sunday

9.00 am	**Sports on Sunday morning –** *Saturday's football matches*
10.30 am	**The World Today –** *A look at new science*
12.00 pm	**The Weather**

2a Change the order of the words in the sentences below. Make questions. Look at the conversation for help.

1 **+**

| He | is | going to | watch TV. |

?

| | | | |

2+ **+**

| They | are | going to | watch TV. |

?

| | | | |

b Now complete the short answers for **going to**.

Yes, she _____ .

you _____ .

No, she _____ .

you _____ .

CHECK YOUR ANSWERS AND STUDY THE CHARTS ON PAGE 70.

3 Match the questions and answers. Complete the questions.

1 Are they going to watch *Nature Watch?*

2 _____ do his homework?

3 _____ go to the party?

4 _____ do any sport next weekend?

5 _____ fly to Turkey?

1 [d] 2 [ ] 3 [ ] 4 [ ] 5 [ ]

a No, she's shy. She doesn't like parties.

b Yes, they are. They always play basketball on Saturdays.

c No, I'm not. I don't like aeroplanes.

d Yes, they are. They love animals.

e No, he isn't. He's lazy.

TOMORROW

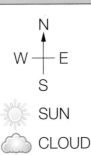

N
W —|— E
S

☀ SUN
☁ CLOUD
🌧 RAIN
❄ SNOW

WEEKEND

5 Use your answers in exercise 4 and write questions about the weather at the weekend. Then use the weekend map and write answers.

1 Is it going to be cloudy in the east?
  No, it isn't. It's going to be sunny.
2 _____
  _____
3 _____
  _____
4 _____
  _____

4 Look at the weather map for tomorrow. Answer the questions.

1 Where is it going to be cloudy tomorrow?
  It's going to be cloudy in the east.
2 Where is it going to rain?

3 Where is it going to snow?

4 Where is it going to be sunny?

6 Read the conversation and complete the questions.
Use **What**, **When**, **Where** and **Who**.

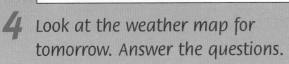

I'm going to go on holiday next summer.

1 _____ ?
  To Bodrum in Turkey. It's beautiful.

2 _____ ?
  In July or August.

3 _____ with?
  With Mum and Dad and two friends.

4 _____ ?
  I'm going to sit in the sun, lie on the beach and swim in the sea.

7 What are you going to do on your next school holiday? Write four sentences.

1 _____
2 _____
3 _____
4 _____

PUZZLE

The weather man is going to draw six lines on the weather map, and make eight parts. All the parts are going to be the same size. They are all going to have sun and rain in each part. How is he going to do it? Draw the lines.

21 Who were they?

1a Read the text about the first people.

There were people in Africa 2 million years ago. Who were they? Scientists call them Homo habilis. It means 'handy man' (with useful hands!). Homo habilis weren't tall, about 1.3 m, and they were hairy and strong. Their lives were short. They were hunters and the world was a dangerous place!

Were Homo habilis clever? We don't know, but their brains were small – about 700 ml. Today, a person's brain is about 1400 ml.

brain

b Is the text talking about people in the past, present or future? _____

2a Match the forms of **be** below.

be present	*be* past
is •	• were
isn't •	• weren't
are •	• wasn't
aren't •	• was

b Put the words below in the correct order and make sentences.

1 | were | Where | they | from | ? |
_____

2 | from | They | Africa | were |
_____

3 | they | Were | tall | ? |
_____

4 | No, | weren't | they |
_____

CHECK YOUR ANSWERS AND STUDY THE CHARTS ON PAGE 70.

3 Write affirmative or negative sentences about **yesterday**.

1 _____She was_____ cold.

2 _____ snowy.

3 _____ happy.

4 _____ any buses.

5 _____ lucky!

4 Look at the pictures of two ancient wonders of the world. Complete the questions about them.

Colossus

1 _____Was it_____
in Europe?

2 _____
a statue?

3 _____
small?

Hanging Gardens

4 _____
in Africa?

5 _____
by the River Euphrates?

6 _____
the walls strong?

5 Now read the information. Write short answers to the questions in exercise 4.

1 Yes, it was.   4 _____

2 _____   5 _____

3 _____   6 _____

Ancient wonders of the world

Colossus at Rhodes	**Hanging Gardens of Babylon**
2,300 years ago	2,500 years ago
in Greece	in Iraq
metal statue	by the Euphrates
33 m tall	walls: 7 m thick

6 General Knowledge

a Make questions about the people and things.

1 What was the Colossus?

2 _____

3 _____

4 _____

5 _____

6 _____

7 _____

1 The Colossus   2 Cleopatra   3 The Titanic

4 The Wright brothers

5 Martin Luther King

6 The Hanging Gardens

7 Amelia Earhart

b Find the answers to these questions at home.

7 Write answers to the questions about you.

1 Were you at school yesterday?

_____

2 Was it sunny yesterday?

_____

3 Were you ill last winter?

_____

4 Where was your mother at 10 a.m. yesterday?

_____

5 Was your teacher late this morning?

_____

6 Where were you at 7 p.m. yesterday?

_____

PUZZLE

Photo finish: It was a very close race!

Number 7 was second.
Number 9 wasn't first.
Number 2 wasn't last.
Number 18 was third.
What were their places?

First (1st) _____   Second (2nd) _____

Third (3rd) _____   Fourth (4th) _____

51

1a Read the text.

b Are these sentences right or wrong?

1 The ancient Chinese studied science. ☐
2 The Italians invented pasta. ☐
3 The ancient Chinese sailed to Europe. ☐

Where were the first cities?

THERE WERE small cities in the Middle East and North Africa about 8,000 years ago. The first big cities were in China on the Yangtse (Yellow River) 3,500 years ago.

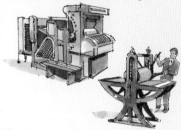

The Chinese started the Great Wall over 2,000 years ago. It's very big – 4,100 km long! The wall stopped dangerous Attila (406 – 453 AD) and the Huns, but it didn't stop Genghis Khan and the Mongols in 1211 AD.

The Chinese studied science. They invented printing 1,000 years ago and then fireworks and guns. They sailed from the Pacific Ocean to Africa.

The Chinese didn't visit Europe, but Marco Polo visited China in 1292 and sailed home to Italy with pasta. The Italians liked it!

2a Is the text talking about the past, present or future? _____

b Match the forms of **do** below.

present simple	past simple
do •	
	• didn't
don't •	
does •	
	• did
doesn't •	

c Complete the past simple affirmative (+) and negative (–) sentences below. Use the text for help.

1 (+) The wall [   ] Attila.
2 (–) It [   ] [   ] Genghis Khan.
3 (+) Marco Polo [   ] China.
4 (–) The ancient Chinese [   ]
[   ] Europe.

3a Match the verbs with their past simple endings. They are all in the text!

start •	• d
stop •	• ed
study •	• ped
like •	• ied

b Write the past simple forms of these verbs.

carry _____   want _____

love _____   stir _____

CHECK YOUR ANSWERS AND STUDY THE CHARTS ON PAGE 71.

4 Complete the sentences. Use the past simple affirmative.

1 Leonardo _painted_ pictures.
2 Marie Curie _____ science.
3 Columbus _____ to America.
4 Beethoven _____ the piano.

Leonardo

Marie Curie

Christopher Columbus

Beethoven

5 Write past simple affirmative and negative sentences about the ancient Chinese.

1 (study/English/science) They didn't study English. They studied science.

2 (listen/music/radio) _____

3 (live/Asia/America) _____

4 (visit/Africa/Europe) _____

5 (cook/rice/burgers) _____

6 (invent/fireworks/TV) _____

6 Complete the text with the past forms of the verbs below. Use the negative form of two verbs.

be   enjoy   invent   live
play   sail   study   visit

The ancient Greeks

(1) _____ over 2,000 years ago.

They (2) _____ clever people. They

(3) _____ mathematics and science.

They (4) _____ their ships to

different countries in the Mediterranean, but

they (5) _____ China or America.

The Greeks (6) _____ playing sports

and they (7) _____ the first Olympic

Games. Today, the Olympic Games is very

different. The ancient Greeks (8) _____

football or basketball!

7 Write sentences about last weekend. Use five different verbs.

Examples:

I studied ... / I didn't study ...

1 _____
2 _____
3 _____
4 _____
5 _____

P U Z Z L E

In 1845, Sophie Strong:
  – studied Portuguese in spring;
  – sailed to Brazil in summer;
  – arrived in Rio in autumn.

What did she do in winter?
a explored the Amazon
b climbed the Andes
c walked across the Atacama desert

53

1a Read the conversation.

PAULO: Did you have a good weekend, James?

JAMES: No, I didn't. I had a terrible weekend. Aunt Flo visited us.

PAULO: Not again! Oh, no!

JAMES: She made a cake, but I didn't eat it. I gave my piece to the dog ... and he ate it! Then he was sick on the chair and Aunt Flo sat in it! She told old stories about the family, she sang old songs and drank hundreds of cups of tea. It was very boring. Dad went out and I went to bed early – at 8.30!

PAULO: When did she go?

JAMES: She didn't go. She enjoyed the weekend and she's going to stay for a week!

b Are these sentences right or wrong?

1 The dog didn't eat the cake. ☐

2 James didn't sing. ☐

3 James's dad stayed in. ☐

2 Look at the conversation. Find the past simple affirmative forms of the verbs below.

1 have _____   6 tell _____

2 make _____   7 sing _____

3 give _____   8 drink _____

4 eat _____   9 go _____

5 sit _____

▶▶▶ CHECK YOUR ANSWERS AND STUDY THE CHARTS ON PAGE 72.

3 Complete Paulo's sentences about his family's visit to the zoo last weekend. Use the verbs below.

fall   give   ~~go~~   ride   see   throw

1 We _went to the zoo._

2 Carlos _____

3 We _____

4 I _____

5 It _____

6 Dad _____ down!

4a Make the sentences below into questions. Then complete the answers.

1 You had a good weekend.

_____

No, _____ didn't.

2 She enjoyed the weekend.

_____

Yes, _____ did.

b Now write Wh- questions for the answers below.

1 _____

She went on Monday.

2 _____

They went to Washington DC.

3 _____

They saw the White House.

⏵⏵ CHECK YOUR ANSWERS AND STUDY THE CHARTS ON PAGE 72.

5 Write questions and answers. Use the correct forms of the verbs.

1 the ancient Chinese / eat / rice / chips
Did the ancient Chinese eat rice?
Yes, they did. They didn't eat chips.

2 the ancient Chinese / drink / tea / coffee

_____

_____

3 dinosaurs / have / big bodies / big brains

_____

_____

4 Attila the Hun / ride / a motorcycle / a horse

_____

_____

5 Columbus / go / Australia / America

_____

_____

6 Write Wh- questions.

ALEXANDRIA
GIZA • CAIRO
• SUEZ
River Nile ASYUT
EDFU • LUXOR
ABU • ASWAN
SIMBEL

1 Who were these people?
They were ancient Egyptians.

2 _____
They lived 5,000 years ago.

3 _____
They lived near the River Nile.

4 _____
They ate bread, meat, fish and vegetables.

5 _____
They made big statues and the Pyramids.

7 Write seven sentences about your day yesterday. Use irregular verbs from the chart in Grammar reference.

1 _____

2 _____

3 _____

4 _____

5 _____

6 _____

7 _____

PUZZLE

Two mothers and two daughters went out on a rainy day. They all had an umbrella. There were only three umbrellas. Explain.

55

24 What team did Pelé play for?

1a Read the questions and answers.

Paulo is answering questions on his special subject, the footballer Pelé, in the school quiz.

What is Pelé's real name? Edson Arantes do Nascimento.
What country did Pelé play for? Brazil.
How many World Cup medals did he win? Three.
When did he win his first World Cup medal? 1958.
How old was he? 18.
What team did he play for in Brazil? He played for Santos.
Why did he go to the USA? He went to the USA because he liked the New York team, Cosmos. Cosmos wanted Pelé for their team.
How many goals did he score altogether? 1,281.

b Are these sentences right or wrong?

1 Pelé didn't play for Brazil.
2 He was from New York.
3 He scored 2,000 goals.

2a Look at the question and answer from the quiz.

Why did he go to the USA?
He went to the USA **because** he liked the New York team, Cosmos.

b Match the phrases below.

1 She's going to the restaurant ...
2 She's running ...
3 She's going to bed ...

a ... because she's late. ☐
b ... because she's tired. ☐
c ... because she's hungry. ☐

c Put the words in the correct order and make the question.

| they | Why | are | running? |

_____

They're running because they're late.

CHECK YOUR ANSWERS ON PAGE 72.

3 Complete the conversation between James and his teacher.

1 Why are you late?
2 Because I missed the bus.
3 Why did you miss the bus?
4 Because I got up late.
5 Why _____ ?
6 _____ I woke up late.
7 _____ ?
8 _____ I went to bed late.
9 _____ ?
10 _____ I watched the eclipse last night.

4a Match the questions and answers below.

1 How old was Pele in 1958?   a 700 ml
2 How tall was the Colossus at Rhodes?   b 33 m
3 How long was the Great Wall of China? c 4,100 km
4 How big was Homo habilis's brain?   d 18

b Put the words in the correct order and make the question.

| high | is | How | Mount Everest | ? |

8,848 m.

c Look at the questions from the quiz again.

8,848m high

What **country** did he play for?
What **team** did he play for in Brazil?
How many **World Cup medals** did he win?

d Put the words below in the correct order and make questions.

1 | play for | did | What | US team | he | ? |

2 | teams | How many | he | did | play for | ? |

CHECK YOUR ANSWERS ON PAGE 72.

5 Write questions about Tyrannosaurus Rex. Use the words below.

heavy ~~long~~ long tall

1 How long was it?   14 m.
2 _____   7 tonnes.
3 _____   6 m.
4 _____
    15 cm.

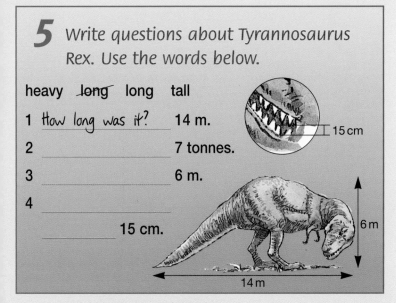

15 cm
6 m
14 m

6 Complete the questions. Use **What** or **How many** and the words below.

books   car   children   ~~languages~~   pets

1 What languages does he speak?
He speaks English, German, French, ...
How many languages does he speak?
Four!

2 _____?
I like horror stories.

3 _____?
We've got six.

_____?
Three cats, two dogs and a mouse.

4 _____?
She drives a VW.

5 _____?
They've got eight but four are married.

7 Answer the questions about you.

1 How many pets have you got?

2 What languages can you speak?

3 How tall are you?

4 How old are you?

PUZZLE

A little boy lives on the tenth floor in a block of flats. Every morning, the boy takes the lift from the tenth floor to the ground. Every evening, he comes home, takes the lift to the fifth floor and gets out. Then he walks up the stairs to the tenth floor. Why does he do this?

57

1 Write questions and answers.

1 What's he going to do?
   He's going to jump in the pool.

2 _____

3 _____

4 _____

5 _____

2 Eric is going to have a party with his friends tomorrow. Kim is asking about it. Look at Eric's list and complete Kim's questions.

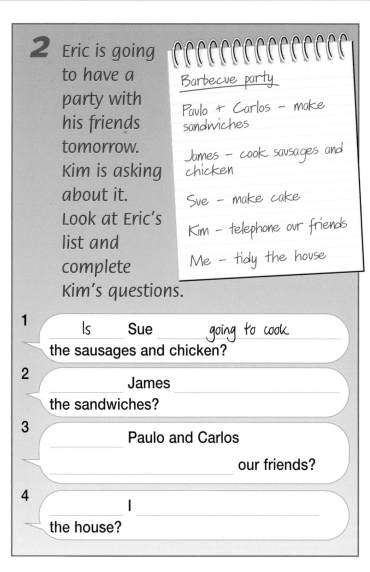

Barbecue party

Paulo + Carlos – make sandwiches

James – cook sausages and chicken

Sue – make cake

Kim – telephone our friends

Me – tidy the house

1 ___Is___ Sue _____ going to cook
   the sausages and chicken?

2 _____ James _____
   the sandwiches?

3 _____ Paulo and Carlos
   _____ our friends?

4 _____ I _____
   the house?

3 Now write Eric's answers to Kim's questions.

1 No she isn't. She's going to make a cake.

2 _____

3 _____

4 _____

4 Write the past simple forms of the verbs.

carry	carried	hate	____	run	____
climb	____	have	____	stay	____
close	____	invent	____	stop	____
come	____	know	____	study	____
do	____	like	____	think	____
go	____	make	____	walk	____

5 Complete the story about the barbecue party with the correct forms of the verbs below. Use the negative form of two or more verbs.

~~be~~ be be be break drop eat go
go have rain run throw watch

The day after the barbecue ...

The friends (1) _____weren't_____ very lucky. Kim
(2) _____ the cassette player, and it
(3) _____ . Then, there
(4) _____ any music. There
(5) _____ a fire on the barbecue and
Paulo (6) _____ water on the
sausages. The dog (7) _____ away
with the chicken and (8) _____ it.
Then it (9) _____ so they
(10) _____ into the house and they
(11) _____ TV. It
(12) _____ boring. They
(13) _____ a
good time.

Next weekend, they (14) _____
_____ to the cinema – no fires, no
dogs and no rain!

6 Write the questions for the question and answer game 'Name the animal'.

1 _____

> It lives in South America.

2 _____

> It eats spiders and flies.

3 _____

> It's about 30 cm long.

4 _____

> It's red.

5 _____

> It's got about a hundred.

> I know! It's a giant centipede!

Grammar reference

1 Hello. You're new here

1b 1 I 2 you 3 she 4 he 5 it
6 we 7 you 8 they 9 they 10 they

2

Be present

affirmative (+)

1	I am = I'm	you are = you're	he is = he's she is = she's it is = it's
2+	we are = we're	you are = you're	they are = they're

4a It's beautiful. It**'s not** friendly.
They**'re not** happy.

b I: 'm not, am not
she, he, it: 's not, isn't, is not
we, you, they: aren't, 're not, are not

Be present

negative (–)

1			2+		
I am not	I'm not		we are not	we're not	we aren't
you are not	you're not	you aren't	you are not	you're not	you aren't
she is not he is not it is not	she's not he's not it's not	she isn't he isn't it isn't	they are not	they're not	they aren't

⚠ ~~I amn't~~

2 Who are you?

1b

| Are | you | OK? |

| Who | is | she? |

Be

questions (?)

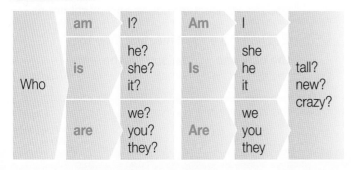

short answers

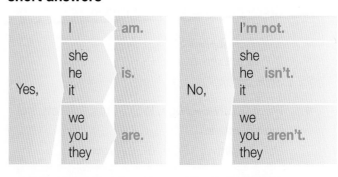

Use *who* for questions about a person/people.

3 A star prize! What is it?

1b   1 What is it?   2 What are they?

c   1 (It's) a car(.)
     2 (They're) a computer, an exercise bike, (and) a television(.)

d

| What | is | it? |

Use *what* for a thing/things.
(Use *who* for a person/people.)

2b   dishes, babies, bags, cakes

4a   a camera   an **e**xercise bike
       a television   an **a**larm clock

b   Look at the first letter of the words.
Use *an* with *a-, e-, i-, o-, u-* (vowels):

an **a**pple   an **e**lephant   an **i**ce cream

an **o**range   an **u**mbrella

Use *a/an* with singular nouns, <u>not</u> with plural nouns.

Plural nouns – spelling rules

+ *-s*	For words with *-y*		For words with *-f* or *-fe*
camera cameras	~~y~~ + *-ies*		~~f~~ or ~~fe~~ + *-ves* 
computer + *-s* computers	baby + *-ies* babies		wolf + *-ves* wolves
bag bags	story stories		knife knives

+ *-es* for words with *-ch, -sh, -s, -x*	But + *-s* for words with *-a, -e, -i, -o, -u* and *-y*		No rule!
match matches			child children
dish + *-es* dishes	key + *-s* keys		mouse mice
glass glasses			person → people → 
fox foxes	boy boys		sheep sheep
			tooth teeth
			man men
			woman women

4 It's an excellent film!

1b **** = excellent

2a 1 It's an excellent film.
2 It's a great adventure.

b They're great actors.

Correct order = adjective + noun

d 1 She's **a g**ood actor.
2 He's **a f**unny man.
3 It's **an e**xciting adventure.

e For adjective + noun, look at the first letter of the adjective.
Use *an* with *a-, e-, i-, o-, u-* (vowels).

4a *Batman Forever* is **1 an** excellent film!
2 The film's exciting.

b *Batman Forever* is **1 a** great adventure.
2 The adventure is exciting.

c The first time, use *a/an* for singular nouns but <u>not</u> for plural nouns. The second time and after, use *the* for singular nouns <u>and</u> plural nouns.

But use *the* every time, first time too:
the only one   the sun   the sky

5 These are my posters

1b 1 B   2 C   3 A

2

he	his
they	their
it	its
she	her
Kylie	Kylie's

5

	near	far	1	2+
this	✓	✗	✓	✗
these	✓	✗	✗	✓
that	✗	✓	✓	✗
those	✗	✓	✗	✓

1b   1 Babs   2 Clare   3 Al   4 Dave

2

It's my breakfast.	It's **mine**.
It's your breakfast.	It's **yours**.
It's his breakfast.	It's **his**.
It's her breakfast.	It's **hers**.
It's our breakfast.	It's **ours**.
It's their breakfast.	It's **theirs**.
It's Dave's breakfast.	It's **Dave's**.
It's the dog's breakfast.	It's the **dog's**.
It's the dogs' breakfast	It's the **dogs'**.

⚠️ It's ~~its~~.

4a   1 Whose breakfast is this?
       2 Is this yours?

b   1 **Whose** breakfasts **are** those?
       2 **Are** those yours?

Use *whose* for questions about people/animals and their things, friends, family, other people.

Whose desk is this?   **Whose** son is he?

1b   1 Yes, she is.   2 No, they aren't.

2a

I you — has
we they — hasn't
— have
she he it — haven't

b

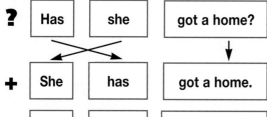

? | Has | she | got a home?
+ | She | has | got a home.
− | She | hasn't | got a home.

c

Have you got a dog? — Yes, I have.
Has he got a dog? — Yes, he has.
— No, he hasn't.
— No, I haven't.

Have got

affirmative (+)

I You We They	have 've		a ball.
		got	
He She It	has 's		

negative (–)

I You We They	haven't 've not		a ball.
		got	
He She It	hasn't 's not		

questions (?)

Have	I you we they	got	a ball?
Has	she he it Tina	got	a ball?

short answers

Yes,	I you we they	have.	No,	I you we they	haven't. 've not.
	she he it	has.		she he it	hasn't. 's not.

8 Are there any comics?

1b   a ✓   b ✗   c ✗

2

	+	–	?
singular (1)	a/an	a/an	a/an
plural (2+)	some	any	any

3

There	is isn't	a bag. an orange.
	are aren't	some comics. any CDs.

Is	there	a bag? an apple?
Are		any watches?

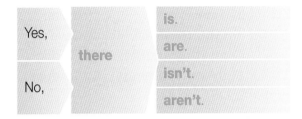

Singular (1) nouns
  Use *there is* + *a/an*.
Plural (2+) nouns
  Use *there are* + *some* with affirmative (+) sentences.
  Use *there aren't* + *any* with negative sentences (–).
  and *are there* + *any* with questions (?).

9 How much orange juice is there?

1b   2 1 litre   4 three

2a   1 There **are** some orange**s**.
2 How **many** orange**s are** there?
3 There **is** some orange juice.
4 How **much** orange juice **is** there?

b   much: sugar, orange juice
many: oranges, glasses

3

Countable nouns	Uncountable nouns
oranges	sugar
apples	bacon
biscuits	chicken
chips	fruit
crisps	tea
bananas	cereal
burgers	coffee
cakes	lemonade
eggs	meat
sandwiches	oil
sausages	water

Use *some* and *any* with uncountable nouns.
  There is **some** orange juice. There isn't **any** orange juice.
  Is there **any** orange juice? Have you got **any** orange juice?

Use *How many ... ?* with countable nouns.
  How many oranges have you got?
  How many oranges **are** there?

Use *How much ... ?* with uncountable nouns.
  How much orange juice have you got?
  How much orange juice **is** there?

Use *How many* for questions about the number of things
and *How much* for questions about the amount of things.

10 What's in your fridge?

1b 2 It's **under** the table.

3 They're **on** the table.

2

on   in   under   behind   between   next to/by/beside   in front of   above

Use *Where* for questions about the places of things.

11 Don't sit in the sun

1b 1 ✓   2 ✗   3 ✓   4 ✗   5 ✓

c don't

2 1 **Drink** lemonade.

2 **Don't** stand in the sun at midday.

Imperatives

affirmative (+)	negative (–)
sit	don't sit / do not sit
stand	don't stand / do not stand
drink	don't drink / do not drink

Use verbs for actions.

Use imperatives for advice, instructions, orders, warnings.

12 What can you do?

1b 1 ✓   2 ✗   3 ✓

c Yes, they can.

2 What **can** they do?

They **can** crawl. They **can't** walk.

Can they run? No, they **can't**.

Can

affirmative (+)			negative (–)		
I You She He It We You They	can	walk. run. understand.	I You She He It We You They	cannot can't	walk. run. understand.

questions (?)

Can	I you she he it we you they	walk? run? understand?	

short answers

Yes,	I you she he it we you they	can.	No,	I you she he it we you they	cannot. can't.

Use *can* for ability.

13 Papuans live in the Pacific

1b A 2   B 3   C 1
     1 ✗   2 ✓   3 ✗

2a   + They **live** in villages.
     – They **don't live** in cities.

b   + They **wear** necklaces.
    – They don't wear school uniforms.

Present simple

affirmative (+)

I You We They Children Papuans	grow eat	vegetables.

negative (–)

I You We They Children Papuans	do not don't	grow eat	necklaces.

Use the present simple for things that happen again and again.

14 Do you play the drums?

1b   3   1   2

2a
1 Do you go to school? → Yes, I do.
2 Where do you go to school? → I go to school in London.
3 When do you go to school? → I go to school in the morning.
4 How do you go to school? → I walk to school.
5 What do you do at school? → I study science.

Use *when* **for time.**
Use *how* **for the way we do things, or the way things happen.**

b
1 **Do** you get up at 7.00?
No, I **don't**.
2 **When do** you get up?
I **get up** at 6.00.

Present simple

questions (?)

Do	I you we they Papuans	walk play study get up	to school? the drums? English? at 7.00?

short answers

Yes,	I you we they Papuans	do.	No,	I you we they Papuans	do not. don't.

5a in → the morning
on → Monday
at → 1.00/2.00

in	on	at
the morning	Monday	1.00/2.00
the afternoon	Tuesday	midday
the evening	Wednesday	midnight
spring	Thursday	the weekend
summer	Friday	night
autumn	Saturday	lunch (time)
winter	Sunday	dinner (time)
January	my birthday	New Year
February	New Year's day	

15 Sometimes he doesn't wake up for school

1c Chris **takes** care of the baby.
Chris **doesn't** wake up for school.

2b

I watch	he watch**es**
I tidy	he tid**ies**
I read	he read**s**
I do	he do**es**

Present simple *he, she, it* (3rd person) – spelling rules

+ -s

read		reads
wear	**+ -s**	wear**s**
like		like**s**

+ -es for words with -ch, -o, -sh, -s, -x or -z

do		does
go	**+ -es**	go**es**
watch		watch**es**
wash		wash**es**

~~y~~ + -ies for words with a consonant + -y

try		tries
fly	**+ -ies**	fl**ies**
tidy		tid**ies**

Present simple

affirmative (+)   negative (–)

She	reads.	She	**does not**	read.
He	go**es** home.	He	**doesn't**	go home.
It	fl**ies**.	It		fly.

questions (?)

| **Does** | she
he
it | read?
go home?
fly? |

short answers

| Yes, | she
he
it | **does.** | No, | she
he
it | **does not.**
doesn't. |

5

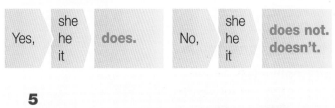

always   usually   often   sometimes   rarely   never
100% ←————————————————————————→ 0%

16 She hates speaking English

1b 1 ✗ 2 ✓ 3 ✗ 4 ✓ 5 ✗

2b

I	me
you	you
she	her
he	him
it	it
we	us
you	you
they	them

4a

dance → dancing
lie → lying
swim → swimming
sing → singing

c

speak	→	speaking	wash →	washing
take	→	taking	make →	making
die	→	dying	tie →	tying
run	→	running	put →	putting

-ing endings – spelling rules

For words with -ie: -ie + -y + -ing   t ie → t ying

For words with -e: -e + -ing   ma ke → mak ing

For words with a vowel and then a consonant
(e.g. -ut, -un, -it), double - × 2 - the consonant + -ing
p ut → put ting

Other words: + -ing

17 They're standing up and shouting

1b 1 B 2 D 3 A 4 C

2
1 They're **playing** football.
2 **Is** the woman watching TV?
No, she**'s not**. / **isn't**. **She's listening** to the radio.
3 **Are** the people shouting?
Yes, they **are**.

Present continuous

affirmative (+)

I	am / 'm	
She He It	is / 's	playing football. shouting. running.
We You They	are / 're	

negative (–)

I	am not / 'm not	
She He It	is not / isn't / 's not	playing football. shouting. running.
We You They	are not / aren't / 're not	

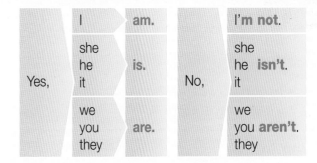

Am	I		
Is	she he it	play**ing**? shout**ing**? run**ning**?
Are	we you they	

short answers

	I	am.			I'm not.
Yes,	she he it	is.	No,	she he it	isn't.
	we you they	are.		we you they	aren't.

Use the present continuous for now.

18 What is James doing?

1b 1 looks   2 is looking

c past now future   past now future

⟶ ○ ⊖ | ○ ○ →   ⟶ ⊕ →

looks   is looking

2a 1 What is James doing?
2 Where is James sitting?

b 1 He's looking at the moon.
2 He's sitting in his bedroom.

19 You're going to be busy!

1b future

2a 1 is going to come
2 aren't going to have

b 1 You aren't going to have any free time.
2 You're going to be busy.
3 You are going to have a good week.
4 You aren't going to have a bad week.

---

be going to

affirmative (+)

I'm		
She's He's It's	going to	get up. eat lunch. go.
You're We're They're		

negative (–)

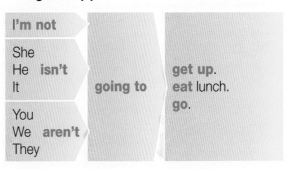

I'm not		
She He isn't It	going to	get up. eat lunch. go.
You We aren't They		

Use *be* + *going to* + verb for the future.

20 *What are you going to watch?*

1b Nature Watch   The Thing 3

2a 1 Is he going to watch TV?
     2 Are they going to watch TV?

be going to

questions (?)

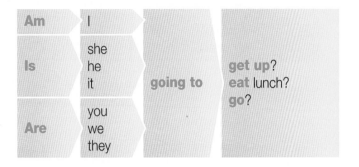

Am	I		
Is	she he it	going to	get up? eat lunch? go?
Are	you we they		

Who What Where How When	am is are	I she he it you we they	going to	visit?

short answers

Yes,	I	am.
	she he it	is.
	you we they	are.

No,	I	'm not.
	she he it	isn't.
	you we they	aren't.

21 *Who were they?*

1b past

2a

be present	*be* past
is	were
isn't	weren't
are	wasn't
aren't	was

b 1 Where were they from?
   2 They were from Africa.
   3 Were they tall?
   4 No, they weren't.

be past

affirmative (+)

I She He It	was	happy.
You We They	were	

negative (–)

I She He It	was not wasn't	happy.
You We They	were not weren't	

questions (?)

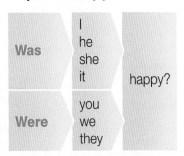

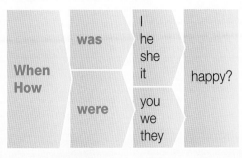

short answers

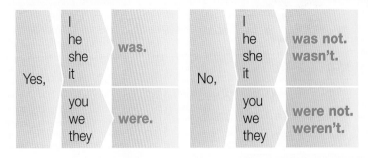

22 They invented printing

1b   1 ✓   2 ✗   3 ✗

2a   past

b
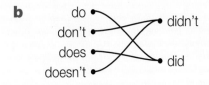

do — didn't
don't — didn't
does — did
doesn't — did

c
1 + stopped
2 – didn't stop
3 + visited
4 – didn't visit

3a
start — d
stop — ed
study — ped
like — ied

b
carry – carried
love – loved
want – wanted
stir – stirred

Past simple regular verbs – spelling rules
Words with -y: -y̶ + -ie + -ed   studied, carried
Words with -e: + -d   liked, loved
Words with a vowel and then a consonant (for example: -ir, -op, -ip), double – × 2 – the consonant + -ed   stirred, stopped
Other words: + -ed   started, looked, watched

Past simple

affirmative (+)

I / You / She / He / It / We / They   stopped. / started. / studied.

negative (–)

I / You / She / He / It / We / They   did not / didn't   stop. / start. / study.

Use the past simple for things in the past.

1b   1 ✗   2 ✓   3 ✗

2   1 had   2 made   3 gave

      4 ate   5 sat   6 told

      7 sang   8 drank   9 went

Past simple

irregular verbs

break	**broke**	read	**read**
catch	**caught**	ride	**rode**
come	**came**	run	**ran**
do	**did**	say	**said**
drink	**drank**	shake	**shook**
drive	**drove**	sing	**sang**
eat	**ate**	sit	**sat**
fall	**fell**	sleep	**slept**
fly	**flew**	speak	**spoke**
get up	**got up**	stand	**stood**
give	**gave**	swim	**swam**
go	**went**	take	**took**
grow	**grew**	tell	**told**
have	**had**	think	**thought**
hit	**hit**	throw	**threw**
keep	**kept**	understand	**understood**
know	**knew**	wake up	**woke up**
make	**made**	win	**won**
meet	**met**	write	**wrote**
put	**put**		

4a   1 Did you have a good weekend?

       No, I didn't.

      2 Did she enjoy the weekend?

       Yes, she did.

b   1 When did she go?

      2 Where did they go?

      3 What did they see?

Past simple

questions (?)

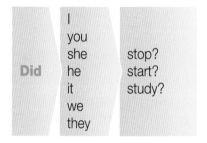

short answers

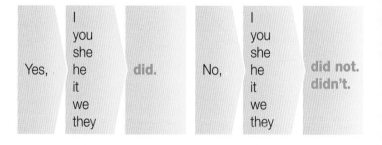

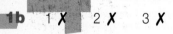

1b   1 ✗   2 ✗   3 ✗

2b   1 She's going to the restaurant **because** she's hungry. [c]

      2 She's running **because** she's late. [a]

      3 She's going to bed **because** she's tired. [b]

c   **Why** are they running?

Use *why* to ask about reasons for things.
Use *because* to explain.

4a   1 d   2 b   3 c   4 a

b   How high is Mount Everest?

d   1 What US team did he play for?

      2 How many teams did he play for?

Wordlist

Write the meanings or other notes for the words below

n = noun
v = verb
adj = adjective
adv = adverb

	Meaning		Meaning		Meaning

a

a 3

about 22

above 10

actor 4

add 11

adventure 4

aeroplane 14

Africa 22

ago 21

alarm clock 3

altogether 24

always 15

America 13

American(s) 13

an 3

ancient 21

and 1

angry 4

answer (v) 16

ant 4

any 8

apple 3

arrive 22

ask 16

at 14

August 14

Australia 13

Australian(s) 13

autumn 14

axe 8

b

baby 3

back (n) 12

bacon 6

bad 7

bag 3

ball 6

banana 9

bank 10

baseball 13

basketball 14

beach 16

beans 6

beautiful 1

because 24

bed 5

bedroom 5

before 18

behind 10

beside 10

between 10

big 13

bike 3

bin 10

biscuit 9

black 8

block 24

block of flats 24

blood 13

blue 3

board 17

boat 5

body 23

book 6

bookshop 10

boring 23

bottle 9

box 8

boy 2

brain 21

brave 2

Brazil 13

Brazilian(s) 13

break (v) 19

breakfast 6

bridge 10

Britain 13

British 2

broken 7

brother 5

brush (v) 15

burger 6

bus 13

bus stop 10

busy 1

by 10

c

café 10

cake 3

call (v) 21

camel 13

camera 3

Canada 13

Canadian(s) 13

car 6

car park 8

Caribbean 11

carnival 16

carrot 11

carrot juice 11

carry 15

cassette 8

cat 2

catch (v) 19

CD 5

cereal 13

chair 5

check (v) 18

chicken 5

child 3

Chinese 12

chips 6

cinema 15

city 3

class 14

classroom 11

clean (v) 16

clearly 12

clever 2

climb 12

clock 3

clothes 17

cloudy 20

coat 17

coconut 13

coffee 9

cold (adj) 14

collect 13

colour 19

column 8

come 14

comic 8

computer 3

computer games 11

cook (v) 15

cooker 10

cool 8

country 14

cow 5

cowboy 13

crawl 12

crazy 2

crisps 9

cupboard 8

d

dad 6

dance 12

dangerous 4

daughter 7

dentist 18

desert 13

desk 5

dictionary 3

die 16

different 22

dinner 17

dirty 1

dish 3

do 11

doctor 18

dog 4

draw 17

dress 6

drink 11

drive 13

drop 11

drum kit 14

drums 14

duck 10

e

each 9

early 23

east 20

eat 11

eclipse 18

egg 6

Egyptians 23

elephant 3

English 14

enjoy 16

Europe 22

evening 14

every 16

excellent 4

	Meaning		Meaning		Meaning

exciting 4

exercise bike 3

expensive 1

explore 22

f

fall (v) 19

farmer 5

fast 1

father 18

feel 17

fifth 24

film 4

finally 11

finger 7

fireworks 22

first 11

fish (n) 6

fish (v) 13

fishing rod 6

flat 7

fly (v) 13

focus 12

food 14

football 13

forest 13

fourteen 2

fourth 21

fox 3

free time 19

French 14

Friday 14

fridge 10

friendly 1

frightening 4

fruit 11

fruit juice 11

funny 4

g

game 17

garden 7

German 24

get up 14

girl 2

give 16

glass 3

glove 6

go 13

go out 19

goal 17

good 4

goodbye 17

gorilla 12

gram 9

grandma 16

grandmother 16

grandparents 7

grass 11

great 4

Greek(s) 22

green (adj) 19

ground 24

grow 13

guitar 13

gun 22

h

hairy 21

handy 21

happy 1

hard 15

hardworking 4

hat 6

hate 16

headache 7

heavy 24

hello 1

help (v) 15

here 1

high 24

history 14

holiday 11

home 5

homework 11

horror film 20

horror story 24

horse 5

hot 1

house 7

housework 15

how 14

how many 9

how much 9

hundreds 23

hungry 1

hunt 13

hunter 21

husband 15

i

ice 11
ice cream 3
ice cream maker 3
ill 1
in 10
in front of 10
information 16
interesting 19
into 11
invent 22
inventor 5
Italian(s) 13
Italy 13

j

jogging 15
journey 15
jug 10
juice 9
July 14
jump (v) 19

k

keep 13
key 3
kick (v) 19
kitchen 10
knife 3
know 14

l

language 13
last 21

late 21
lazy 4
learn 13
left 11
leg 7
lemon 11
lemonade 9
leopard 4
letter 16
lie 16
life 19
lift (n) 8
like 13
line 20
lion 2
listen 11
litre 9
litter 11
live 13
long 17
look 17
love 16
lucky 19
lunch 14

m

mad 16
magazine 8
make 13
man 3
married 24
match 3
mathematics 22
maths 14

mean (v) 21
meat 9
medal 24
meet 15
metal 21
metre 4
midday 11
Middle East 22
million 21
mine 6
miss (v) 24
model 13
Monday 14
Mongol(s) 13
Mongolia 13
Mongolian(s) 13
month 12
moon 18
morning 14
mosquito 13
mother 5
motorbike 13
motorcycle 23
mountain 13
mouse 3
mouth 7
move 11
mum 6
music 5
musical instrument 13

n

name 5
necklace 13

neighbour 14

never 15

new 1

newborn 12

newsagent 10

next 11

next to 10

no 1

north 20

North Africa 22

nose 7

not 1

not bad 4

o

officer 17

often 15

oil 9

old 1

on 10

on fire 18

one 12

only 5

open (v) 19

orange 3

orange juice 9

over 22

p

Pacific 13

Pacific Ocean 22

paint (v) 13

Papua New Guinea 13

Papuan(s) 13

parents 13

park 10

part 20

party 3

past 17

pasta 22

pattern 11

pen 3

people 3

person 3

personality 4

personality test 4

pet 7

phone (n) 19

photo 11

piano 14

picture 12

piece 23

pig 5

pineapple 11

pineapple juice 11

pizza 13

place 21

planet 18

plate 10

play 11

police 17

Portuguese 22

post box 10

post office 10

poster 5

pour 11

practise 14

printing 22

prize 3

professor 16

programme 20

project 16

put 11

q

quiz 24

r

radio 8

rain 20

rarely 15

read 12

red 3

restaurant 8

ride 12

right (adj) 1

right (adv) 11

river 10

road 13

row (n) 8

run 11

s

sail (v) 22

same 20

sandwich 9

Saturday 14

sausage 9

say 12

scarf 6

school 7

school uniform 11

	Meaning		Meaning		Meaning

science 14

scientist 21

score 24

sea 13

second 21

see 12

serious 4

shampoo 9

sheep 3

shirt 6

shoe 6

shop 8

shopping 15

short 1

shout 17

shy 19

sick 23

sing 12

singer 5

sister 15

sit 11

size 20

skates 6

sky 18

sleep (v) 18

slow 1

small 21

smell 12

snow 20

snowy 21

soap 9

sock 6

some 8

sometimes 15

song 5

sore 7

sorry 1

south 20

South America 16

speak 12

special 13

spider 2

spoon 10

spring (n) 14

square 8

squeeze 11

stadium 17

stairs 24

stamp 13

stand 11

stand up 17

star 3

star prize 3

start 14

statue 21

stay up 18

stir 11

stomach-ache 7

stone 13

stop (v) 22

story 3

strong 2

study 14

stupid 2

sugar 9

summer 14

sun 4

sun cream 11

Sunday 14

sunglasses 11

sunny 20

sweet 7

swim 12

swimming pool 8

t

take 11

take care of 15

tall 1

taste 12

tea 9

teacher 11

team 24

teddy 6

telephone (n) 8

telephone (v) 16

telescope 5

television 3

tennis 12

tent 13

tenth 24

terrible 14

test 4

that 5

the 3

them 16

then 11

these 5

thick 21

think 14

	Meaning		Meaning		Meaning

third 21

thirteen 1

this 5

those 5

three 3

throw (v) 19

Thursday 14

tidy (adj) 4

tidy (v) 14

tie (v) 16

tired 1

toast 6

today 1

tomorrow 20

tonight 18

tooth 3

toothache 7

toothpaste 9

tree 12

Tuesday 14

turn 11

TV 4

two 4

u

ugly 2

umbrella 3

uncle 14

under 10

underground 5

understand 12

unfriendly 4

untidy 4

use 11

useful 21

usually 15

v

vegetable 13

very good 4

video 6

village 13

visit 16

w

wait 18

wake up 15

walk (n) 14

walk (v) 11

wall 14

want 16

wash 11

watch (n) 3

watch (v) 13

water 9

wear 11

weather 20

weather man 20

weather map 20

Wednesday 14

week 12

weekend 19

west 20

what 3

when 14

white 8

who 2

whose 6

why 24

wife 7

wild 5

win 3

window 19

winter 14

wolf 3

woman 3

wonder (n) 21

word 12

work 7

world 21

write 12

wrong 1

y

year 12

yes 1

your 5

yours 6

z

zoo 3

Thanks and acknowledgements

I would especially like to thank the editorial team at Cambridge University Press, in particular Jeanne McCarten, Nóirín Burke, Bella Wigan and Liz Driscoll for their encouragement, patience and invaluable help. I would also like to thank the design team, especially Marcus Asquith and Samantha Dumiak, for their astonishing creativity. Finally, a deeply heartfelt thanks to Alison Sharpe for all her support and sensitivity when most needed.

Many thanks also to the following teachers, students and institutions from all over the world who reviewed and pilot-tested material from *Grammar Works 1*: Margaret Allen, Instituto Británico, Segovia, Spain; María Teresa Aracena, Santiago, Chile; Irene Barros Villar, La Coruña, Spain; Carlos Barbisan, São Paulo, Brazil; Sarah Brierley, Cambridge, UK; Jamie Carrera, Santiago, Chile; Esteban Cresta, Buenas Aires, Argentina; Roberta Facchinetti, University of Bergamo, Italy; Ebe Fumagalli Bastos, São Paulo, Brazil; Gabriela Goycoolea Dunalastair, Santiago, Chile; Helen Gravanis, Athens, Greece; Simon Himbury, Hilderstone College, Tokyo, Japan; Rosemary Hurst, Wigan, UK; Kosteleczhi Janosne, Budapest, Hungary; Borbala Juhasz, Budapest, Hungary; Grazyna Kanska, Warsaw, Poland; Anastasía Lakioti tou Christo, Athens, Greece; Claudia Theresa Méndez, Rio de Janeiro, Brazil; Suzana Monteleone Lachowski, São Paulo, Brazil; María Cruz Mozo, Santander, Spain; Adriana Signoretto Martinelli, Scuola Media Luigi Mayno, Milan, Italy; Daniella Mazza, Scuola Media Giovanni XXIII, Milan, Italy; Gulyasne Pustai Reka, Budapest, Hungary; Anna Sikorzynska, Warsaw, Poland; Puangchan Srirakit, Bangkok, Thailand; Maria Jesus Torrealday Zabala , E.U. de Magisterio, Bilbao, Spain; Wayne Trotman, Özel Cakabey Koleji, Izmir, Turkey.

Mick Gammidge, March 1998.

The publishers are grateful to the following for permission to reproduce copyright material. It has not always been possible to identify the sources of all the material used and in such cases the publishers would welcome information from the copyright owners.

For permission to reproduce photographs and other copyright artwork:

Wane Brothers/The Kobal Collection for page 7, Batman (top left) and page 10, Batman (top); Creation Records for page 7, Oasis (top left); Warner Brothers for page 7, Tom & Jerry (bottom left); Glyn Kirk/Action Plus Photographic for page 7, Tiger Woods (bottom left); One Little Indian Records for page 7, Björk (bottom left); Volkswagen Press for page 8, car (top right); Cambridge University Press for page 8, three dictionaries (top right); Daniel J, Cox/Oxford Scientific Films for page 12, foxes (top left); Wallace & Grommit Ltd, /Aardman for page 12, Wallace & Grommit (top left and bottom left); Lynn Goldsmith/Corbis for page 12, Kylie Minogue (top left and bottom left); Chris Matusek/Battersea Dogs' Home for page 18, dog (top right); The Board of Trustees of the University of Illinois for page 29, wife and mother-in-law ambiguous figure (bottom right) and Oxford University Press for page 29, duck/rabbit ambiguous figure (bottom right) from *Seeing – Illusion, Brain and Mind* by John P. Frisby © Oxford University Press (1979); © Best Magazine for page 36, Chris Herbert (top left); Sue Cunnigham Photographic for page 38, Rio (bottom left); Joel Photography for page 49, Bodrum (bottom left); Corbis-Bettman for page 51, The Wright Brothers and Amelia Earhart (centre right); Flip Schulke/Corbis for Martin Luther King Jn. (centre right); Alan Wetton for page 52, Great Wall of China (top right); Peter Robinson/Action Plus Photographic for page 56, Pele (top right).

We would like to thank the following for pictures taken on commission for Cambridge University Press:

Michael Brooke for page 8, objects (top right); Graham Portlock for page 20, objects (top left) and girl (top right).

Illustrations:

Gerry Ball, Phil Burrows, Phil Healey, David Mitcheson, Peter Richardson, Jamie Sneddon, Sam Thompson, Kath Walker, Celia Witchard.

Produced by Gecko Limited, Bicester, Oxon